Vintage Kitchenalia

Emma Kay

AMBERLEY

Decorative ginger jar, *c.* 1825.

First published 2017

Amberley Publishing
The Hill, Stroud
Gloucestershire, GL5 4EP

www.amberley-books.com

British Library Cataloguing in Publication Data.
A catalogue record for this book is available from the British Library.

ISBN 978 1 4456 5751 6 (paperback)
ISBN 978 1 4456 5752 3 (ebook)

Typeset in 9.5pt on 12pt Sabon.
Typesetting and Origination by Amberley Publishing.
Printed in the UK.

Contents

Acknowledgements

As always thank you to everyone at Amberley Publishing for making this book happen and a special thank you this time to Publicity Manager Hazel Kayes, who always secures me fantastic publicity.

My husband Nick Kay, is a truly wonderfully talented photographer. A jolly big thanks goes to him for re-photographing many of the items in my collection to look interesting and far removed from some of the one-dimensional stock photographs that appear in some anthologies. He spent many a rainy and sunny day scouring the Cotswolds for inspirational shots to act as a background for the objects themselves. Without his photographs the book would have been a very different product indeed.

Thanks also go to my gorgeous five-year-old son, who is always so congenial about forsaking special time with me, in order that I get the book written.

In fact, my family in general, which seems to grow bigger every year, have always been supportive and kind and I thank them all for that.

One last word to all those private collectors and lovers of Kitchenalia out there who have written about this subject and have helped me in the process of learning so much more about this fascinating area of social history. And of course you, the readers.

About the Author

Emma Kay is a historian and writer. She has worked as a museum professional for twenty years in institutions including the National Maritime Museum, the British Museum and the University of Bath. She has a degree in History, postgraduate certificate in Roman Archaeology, MA in Heritage Interpretation and a diploma in Cultural Heritage Management. She is a collector of antique and vintage kitchenalia and writes and speaks about the history of cooking and dining to a variety of audiences. Her other books for Amberley Publishing include *The Georgian Kitchen* and *Dining with the Victorians*. She lives in the Cotswolds, England.

Preface

This book is designed to be a reference for all those people who are keen to learn how their everyday kitchen objects evolved and why. How many varieties are there, and who developed them? The many photographs of my collection within, I hope, will also be able to contextualise the objects to a greater extent. Above all I hope readers will find the book a useful and practical tool with which to study items in the kitchen. In the early days of my research, I found it hard to find material on this subject area, particularly material relating to the British kitchen. There are a number of American guides and although there are similarities between the two kitchen histories, the United States had periods of greater progression in this area, alongside a number of very different objects that reflected their own cultural heritage, including the early New Englanders.

It is important to note that this book is far from being a complete compendium of kitchenalia. There are so very many variations of some objects throughout history and of course many objects that I have omitted, for reasons relating to actual book space or simply because they just weren't appropriate for a general anthology.

One of the hardest things about writing this book was how to classify the objects. For instance, should an ice-cream scoop be included in dairy or utensils, and should cake and biscuit moulds go into bakery or the specific chapter on moulds? If I have confused any readers with my choice of categorisation, I unreservedly apologise. I have simply chosen to contextualise items according to my own inherent understanding of what they represent and in accordance with how I catalogue my own private collection of objects.

The majority of the photographs in this book are of items from my own collection of kitchenalia, which I started over ten years ago, inspired by a gift of a 1950s Denby Ware dinner service from a friend. As someone with a passion for the past, I have always loved antiques and surrounding myself with beautiful objects. Given this romantic urge, combined with my own personal love affair with food, it isn't hard to understand how I ended up acquiring some one hundred and fifty odd items of kitchen collectibles.

This is my third book with Amberley Publishing, the previous two – *Dining with the Georgians* and *Dining with the Victorians* – hopefully speak for themselves as comprehensive food history anthologies of two distinct periods in culinary evolution.

Vintage Kitchenalia was an idea for a book we discussed early on in my relationship with Amberley, in accordance with the breadth of knowledge and kitchenalia I have accumulated over the years. There are a few publications dedicated to this area of collecting, many of which are American. The United States has a much broader appreciation of culinary history and it is legitimised there as more of an important theme of social history. Despite Britain's obsession with food and food media, there is a huge gap in the research in this field. By writing and speaking publicly, as I do, and continuing to collect, I hope to be able to raise more awareness of this fascinating area of untapped history.

If you would like to find out more about my work then please do visit https://britishhistoryoffood.com/ and get in touch.

Edwardian silver-plated muffin dish. (Emma Kay)

Introduction

We may live without poetry, music, and art
We may live without conscience, and live without heart;
We may live without friends; we may live without books;
But civilized man cannot live without cooks.
He may live without books – what is knowledge but grieving?
He may live without hope – what is hope but deceiving?
He may live without love – what is passion but pining?
But where is the man that can live without dining?

From *Lucile*, Edward Bulwer-Lytton (1860)

Kitchenalia is a word that has become a collective term for a variety of items used in cooking and dining. History reveals that such items have often been treasured and revered; left in wills, given as wedding gifts, travelled with kings, and the number of incidents of theft of items of kitchenalia recorded in the archives of the Old Bailey is also testament to their value and popularity.

Invention has also always had a strong connection to kitchenware. Once the late Georgians began to appreciate the possibility of satisfying the need for labour-saving devices, in part due to technological advancement, it seems the trend to invent for the kitchen has not slowed down since. There are literally tens of thousands of patents from the mid-1800s to the 1960s, all for items specifically designed to make life easier in the kitchen. Whilst these items would once have been touted and retailed across the country during fairs and expos, and a growing number of cookery demonstrations, kitchen gadgets today still capture the imagination and wallet contents during the annual national food shows, where you can find celebrity and television chefs endorsing them up and down the aisles.

As much as the eighteenth and nineteenth centuries were associated with immigration to Britain, similar numbers of British citizens also emigrated, particularly as sea travel for civilians began to become a possibility. If you possessed a useful trade such as being a domestic servant or an agricultural worker, passage to Australia and America was often 'free', in that you would be guaranteed work or support on arrival. For others, a payment of twenty shillings (about £1,500 in today's money) was requested by the country's commissioners during the mid to latter half of the nineteenth century. This would secure three things on entering the country – a bed, bedding, and cookery utensils.

Those choosing to remain in Britain from the eighteenth century onwards would witness one of the country's greatest transitions in the development of domestic wares. The following list of kitchen items was recorded in 1744, taken from a weaver's cottage in Colchester. Immediately, it gives an understanding of the transition from medieval to post-Enlightenment scientific revolution, as earthenware sits alongside glass and the presence of tin begins to outshine wood.

> Earthenware pans, stew pans, dishes, butter plates, spoons, glasses, mortars, an earthenware jug to be submerged and boiled to make jugged hare, cups, gravy boats, pots, wooden bowls, whisks, tin pans, sieves, basins, kettles, strainers, pie plates, skewers.

Wedgewood's creamware was particularly popular at this time, so you might expect to have also found a teapot and caddy, and as well as a punch bowl and a coffee pot. The fireplace would have been a basic open fire, fuelled by coal and fitted with a turn spit.[1]

If we move forward to the time of the French celebrity chef invasion of Britain, Alexis Soyer – one of the most popular, written-about chefs of the era – included a compilation of essential items for the kitchen in his 1849 edition of *The Modern Housewife*. His list looks quite different from the list one hundred years earlier and includes:

> 8 copper stew pans; two larger ones holding one gallon and a half and the next one gallon, the others smaller by degrees to one pint. 1 oval fish kettle holding about one gallon and a half but if by chance I have a turbot I borrow a kettle from the fishmonger. 1 middle sized braising pan, 1 pre serving pan, 1 round bowl for beating whites of eggs, 2 saucepans, 1 omelette pan, 1 frying-pan, 1 Bain Marie, 6 saucepans for the sauce, 1 middle sized tin pie mould, 2 tin jelly moulds, 1 tin blanc-mould for fruit, 1 freezing pot with every requisite, 2 baking sheets, 1 gridiron, 1 small salamander, 1 colander spoon, 1 bottle jack, 2 spits, 1 dripping pan 1, screen, 1 sugar pan, 2 soup ladles, 8 copper spoons, 2 of them colanders, 2 wire baskets, 1 wire sieve, 2 hair sieves, 24 tartlet pans, 2 tammies, 1 jelly bag, 12 wooden spoons, 2 paste brushes, 1 pair of scissors, 2 kitchen knives, 6 larding needles, 1 packing needle, 1 box of vegetable cutters, 1 box of paste cutters, 1 meat saw, 1 cutlet chopper, 1 meat chopper, 6 meat hooks tinned, 1 rolling pin, 8 kitchen basins, 6 china pie dishes, 6 earthen bowls for soups and gravies, 4 kitchen table cloths, 18 rubbers, 12 fish napkins, 6 pudding cloths, 4 round towels.[2]

Just fifty years later, in 1919, the recommended list is even more diverse. There is now a sense of the kitchen becoming a much more complicated place.

EQUIPMENT OF A KITCHEN FOR A HOUSEHOLD OF ABOUT SIX PERSONS:

Plate rack	2 iron saucepans (different sizes)
Pastry board and rolling pin	1 enamelled saucepan
Chopping board	1 aluminium saucepan or another
Bread board	enamelled pan

1 enamelled preserving pan
1 fish-kettle for boiling fish (Not necessary, Just useful)
ham and large joints.
1 3-tiered steamer, or a steamer to fit one of the saucepans
1 iron frying-pan
1 omelette pan
1 double milk pan. (Not necessary, as a jug or jar may be used in a saucepan)
2 or 3 casseroles (various sizes)
1 large kettle
1 small ditto
1 flour dredger
1 bread and suet grater
1 set of skewers
1 mincing machine
1 colander
2 strainers (1 fine; 1 coarse)
1 fish slice
1 wire sieve. (These are necessary for nice cooking)
1 hair sieve
1 set of scales and weights (Not absolutely necessary)
1-pint measure
1 bread crock
1 flour mug, or barrel
2 or 3 kitchen knives and forks
2 tablespoons
1 dessert spoon
2 teaspoons
1 enamelled soup ladle (Not absolutely necessary)
3 wooden spoons
1 large iron spoon
1 egg whisk
2 large milk basins
Set of various sized basins
China jelly mould

1 tin pudding mould
3 or 4 fireproof dishes. 6 plates for larder
1 cake tin
12 patty pans
12 small cake tins
1 tin opener
1 corkscrew
1 meat chopper
1 vegetable peeler (Not necessary)
1 apple corer (combined, labour saving)
2 Yorkshire pudding tins
1 baking sheet
1 baking tin and trivet
Dish cloths
Netted mop
Drying cloths
Oven cloths
Dusters
Floor cloth. Flannel
Pan brush
Scrubbing brush
Wire pan scrubber
1 long-handled soft broom
1 long-handled scrubber
1 yard brush (To save kneeling)
1 bucket and mop
1 floor cloth.
Zinc bath for washing-up or large enamelled basin
2 buckets
2 black lead brushes
1 cinder sifter
1 flue brush
1 hearth brush
1 coal box
Set of fire irons
1 fire rake
1 fender
1 knife board or knife cleaning machine

FOR WEIGHING WITHOUT A WEIGHING MACHINE

Measures for liquids
1 breakfast cup ... 1 pint
1 teacup 1 pint or 1 gill
1 tumbler 5 pint

20 liquid oz. 1 pint: therefore
20 tablespoonfuls 1 pint.
10 ditto. 1 pint.[3]

Alongside this comprehensive list, is another for accessories required if using a gas or electricity cooker and the need for block tin and enamelware.

Whilst Soyer refers to choppers, saws and cutters, the kitchen of 1919 has a peeler, a corer and a mincing machine. Note the reference to convenient labour saving and the unpretentious reminder that some of these early twentieth century items are 'not necessary' (but clearly desirable), particularly if you want to save your knees by investing in a yard brush. The copper and tin items of the Victorian period are also rapidly being replaced by aluminium and enamelware by 1919. The gridirons and salamanders of the previous centuries have also disappeared, along with the need for a bottle jack or spits. Although Soyer's is a far more detailed list of objects, there are more similarities in many ways between Soyer's list and that of the weaver's cottage, although they are a hundred years apart. This is indicative of the significant influences of innovation borne out of late-Georgian modernisation, followed by the huge shift in technological advancement by the end of the Victorian era and again into the Edwardian era. In addition, items such as tin-openers, corkscrews and steamers, which were all innovations of the nineteenth century, had clearly not established themselves as kitchen staples until the twentieth century. This could be attributed to later mass-production and therefore the lower cost of luxury items.

There is a lovely hypothetical discussion between a Dutch oven, saucepan, spit, frying-pan and gridiron in the 1858 book *Inquire within for anything you want to know*. The dialogue demonstrates a modern opinion about their usage in the Victorian kitchen, as the frying-pan tells the saucepan that it is a 'meat-spoiler', which serves only to adulterate the juices of the best joints of meat. The saucepan's retort is to inform the frying-pan that it can only function when it is 'flooded with oil or fat', and that it is so wide that most of the contents of the chimney above often ends up in the food. It is the spit that receives the next roasting (pardon the pun) from the Dutch oven, who announces that this is the cooking device that requires the most attention as it needs to be constantly watched, whilst leaving an 'unsightly gash' through every joint. The Dutch oven is next to be criticised by the retaliating spit, who christens it a 'dummy' with 'a hood like a monk', that also requires constant vigilance by the cook in order to avoid burning the food on one side whilst leaving it uncooked on the other. But it is the gridiron who gets the unanimous torrent of abuse, as a 'thing with six ribs' that always ends up burning the meat at one end, while surrendering the goodness of the other end to the fire. The writer then steps in to remind the reader that all five utensils have their advantages as they offer a variety of cooking methods including baking, broiling, frying, roasting and stewing, without which all of our food would be very bland.[4] To an extent we still use all these basic cookery tools today; the saucepan and frying-pan go without saying, but the Dutch oven is simply an early version of the slow cooker or a sturdy-lidded casserole dish, the griddle can also be found in most modern kitchens or integrated into barbeques, and the spit is frequently visible in every fashionable city high street, roasting chickens on a rotisserie in the window to lure customers in, or at country food fairs and festivals roasting a pig in the traditional manner, with the meat to be served in hearty white baps. Our methods of cooking have not really changed at all; they have simply evolved with technology.

Once the initial kitchen revolution of the late eighteenth and nineteenth centuries had ensued, there was little to distinguish between the contents of Victorian and Edwardian kitchens – with the exception of enamel wear pots and pans, Bakelite goods, steamers, mincing machines, refrigerators and small freezing machines, as well as water filters and better-equipped, less labour-intensive kitchen ranges.

By the mid eighteen-hundreds, public dining was becoming popular and for the wealthier classes it was often more fashionable to dine out than entertain at home. Domestic staff were reducing as class distinctions became less clear and a new working economy evolved out of industrialisation and the rural to urban shift in living. As a consequence, new kitchens were designed on a smaller, more practical scale to accommodate one person, opposed to a team of domestic staff. The food-hungry years of the Second World War meant that women were making do, rather than consuming new kitchen equipment and the post-war rise in labour-saving gadgetry ushered in phenomenal change but also secured the woman's role in the kitchen as the sole domestic labourer. The 1960s and 70s generated some liberation and empowerment for women, and British kitchens remained the playground of technology for many in terms of innovation, as the media bombarded consumers with the latest kitchen gimmicks.

As the preface notes and as will become apparent when reading more, there was undoubtedly a race between America and Britain in terms of invention, patent submissions and advancement generally where the kitchen was concerned. It is important to mention that all metals were in short supply between 1914 and 1918, during the First World War, therefore very few new house wares were developed at this time. There were also a number of hefty trade restrictions in operation, making it almost impossible to determine what emerged first or from where.

This book focuses on the years between 1700 and the 1950s; obviously there is a wide array of kitchen objects that exist outside this period but, as a collector, they are representative of my collection and embody the areas of food and kitchenalia study I am most familiar with.

Late Victorian silver-plated food warmer. (Emma Kay)

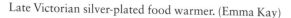

1

Storage

A mahogany truffle box made by one of my old maître d's. It's the most beautiful way
to present fresh truffles to customers during the season.
Michel Roux Jr, Le Gavroche, Roux at Parliament Square, Roux at The Landau, London.
The Guardian, 'I Couldn't Live Without … Top Chefs' Favourite Kitchen Kit', 2011

In the eighteenth century, Susanna Whatman, mistress of the house of Turkey Court
in Kent, who, despite her wealth and class, made it her business to be as involved as
possible in the overall running of the estate, made a list of instructions, observations and
ideas, which made it impossible for any member of the staff to oversee the finer details of
day-to-day housekeeping. This included the storage of kitchen provisions:

> Plenty of sugar should always be kept ready broke in the deep sugar drawers in the
> Closet Storeroom. There is one for spice, one for moist sugar, and two for lump sugar.
> The pieces should be as square as possible, and rather small. The sugar that is powdered
> to fill the silver castor should be kept in a basin in one of the drawers to prevent any
> insects getting into it, and be powdered *fine* in the mortar and kept ready for use.
> Currants and raisins should be kept in a moister place, as in the deep drawers in the
> little cupboard opposite the storeroom. Rice should be ground at leisure times, and kept
> for use. Currant also dried a little before wanted are convenient, as they should be used
> quite dry.[1]

In larger houses the family silver was the responsibility of the butler, and was stored
inside a safe in the butler's pantry. Typically, a footman or the butler himself slept close
to the safe, with a firearm.

Preserving – Salt Boxes and Safes

Salting was and still is an essential method for preserving food, particularly meats and
fish. Salt was added to butter and cheese to both enhance the flavour and increase
longevity. Salt boxes would originally have been taken to the shop to be filled up with
salt. In the late 1700s, it would have cost around sixpence (roughly £1.50 in today's

money) to fill one salt box.[2] There is mention of a Georgian salt box being given as a gift in 1928 to a couple during a famous society wedding in Burnley, illustrating that they were quite prized items.[3]

During the nineteenth century, meats were sometimes preserved in pyroligneous acid. This is wood vinegar, a volatile combination of mostly acetic acid and methanol, sometimes found in cigarettes. Inhalation and contact can frequently trigger skin irritation, skin and eye burns, with inhalation causing dizziness and suffocation. It also produces a highly toxic gas if it comes into contact with fire. Pyroligneous acid was regularly used, as were many other toxic substances such as lime. In fact, pyroligneous acid not only preserved meat, but it could restore it to its former glossy glory, and it was also once widely used in the treatment of leprosy. Meat or fish was either dipped (anything from a few seconds to a minute) into the acid and then dried.[4] Call me fussy but I'm not sure I'd want my T-bone dipped in that.

Often meat was stored in a 'safe', an item that featured in British kitchens from as early as the 1700s until around 1960. Prior to this people would have had to just rely on a 'thrawl', or stone shelf, which was situated in the coolest area of the kitchen or larder. The cool room was known as the 'spence' in Scotland. As the architectural designs for Headfort House in Ireland illustrate, the larder would often be situated in the cellar as the coldest area, with a passage leading to the servants' quarters. Meat safes would come with a lock and in larger houses, the keys were entrusted to both the housekeeper and cook. This, as Susanna Whatman writes in her journal of 1776, was to ensure that the larger cuts of meat were kept away from temptation, 'as it would be difficult to detect depredations on a large joint, and a dishonest servant might contract a habit of doing injustice, and be more difficult to reclaim than when immediate detection follows'.[5]

Spice Boxes

The spice box became popular in Europe during the early 1700s and they were objects often specially commissioned by the wealthy. Craftsmen would create miniature scaled-down versions of tall chests, carve elaborate inlays with double doors and secret drawers within.[6] As the 1800s progressed cheaper boxes emerged made of tin, rather than wood, and by the middle of the nineteenth century 'seasoning boxes' appeared alongside spice boxes. These were cited in essential equipment lists for the kitchen by celebrity chefs of the day, such as Alexis Soyer and Charles Francatelli. Seasoning boxes were often cast as hinged, lidded, tray compartments, on centre pivots, for cooks to easily access the appropriate herbs and spices needed during cooking. It became very popular to Japan these tinned boxes and stamp pretty designs on them, often circular rather than square, presumably to fit in more compartments.

Many storage jars and larger items generally found in the kitchen were enamelled after the First World War, although the process of enamelling – essentially glass bonded onto steel and other metals – started as early as the middle of the eighteenth century in Germany, as a method used to line cooking pots and pans. This made them safer and more hygienic. By the 1940s everything from cups to utensils were enamelled. The white with navy trim of classic British enamelware was applied to buckets, containers and storage items, enabling them to be more durable.

Late eighteenth- to early nineteenth-century spice box. (Emma Kay)

Refrigeration

The story of the refrigerator and its journey to domesticity is both long and complex, and worthy of its own book. Suffice to say that the following is only representative of a small fraction of its evolution.

Iced deserts were extremely fashionable during the Georgian era and it became an enormous task to both maintain a regular supply of ice for this purpose, as well as to prevent food from spoiling. Large estates with lakes would have the gardener extract ice during winter, which would then be stored in brick-built underground ice pits, or caves. Alternatively, 'snow stacks', were constructed by building fenced-off timber areas, laid with bundles of sticks. When it snowed, the snow was thrown into this clearing and trampled underfoot or by horses. Yum. The process continued until it was tightly packed. Rock salt was strewn across the area, then it was covered in thatch. This, believe it or not, could keep a house supplied with ice for around five months of the year.[7] Ice was also available from the fishmonger, via collection or delivery. Fish or seafood for dinner parties would be delivered fresh to avoid inevitable spoiling.

There is an interesting story of French chef, François Vatel who, during a significant banquet whilst in service to Louis XIV, became so distressed by the fact that the seafood delivery was late that he took his own life by running onto his sword. A different version of this story is that it was the dinner component that was delayed. There was a Vatel Society established in America during the 1950s, and a portrayal of the eccentric chef was immortalised in film by Gérard Depardieu in 2000. In the film Vatel kills himself because of his rank, rather than the alleged incident with the seafood.

The earliest form of refrigerators were ice chests or boxes. Basically these were wooden boxes, lined with zinc, then a layer of insulator, such as wood shavings, and topped with

A 1948 refrigerator, featured in an American journal.

Breaking the ice, early 1800s.

another layer of zinc. There was a drainage tap secured to the base. Blocks of ice were placed in the bottom of the box and shelving units placed above to store wine or general provisions. The icebox was then kept in the pantry – a bit like our modern-day cooler bags. By the early twentieth century, the ice compartment was placed on the top of the unit, with the storage cupboard below, and these were still commonly being kept in kitchens right up until the 1950s, although wealthy Britons would have had access to an electric domestic refrigerator as early as the 1920s. The word refrigerator was in common use from the 1850s, along with a wealth of patents and cooling systems using anything from sulphur dioxide to methyl formate – all of which were lethal. One of the first British inventors of refrigeration was William Cullen, as early as 1755.

Cake and Biscuit Tins

Just after the First World War, in Blackburn, there was an epidemic of burglaries that led to the local savings bank being inundated with customers bringing in their cake and biscuit tins full of money to store safely in the vaults. One lady had a biscuit tin 'full to the brim with silver coins', totalling £300 in half-crowns and one lonely florin.[8] In fact throughout the 1930s and '40s there are countless stories relating to stolen money kept in biscuit and cake tins. There was (and often still is) a disdainful attitude amongst the older generation towards banks, preferring instead to hoard life savings in tins and hide them under the bed or on top of cupboards. Understandably, this method of thrifty saving became common knowledge amongst the ne'er-do-wells of society, leading to inevitable multiple thefts and break-ins.

Prior to the nineteenth century as baked goods were cooked and eaten fresh, there was little need for storage containers to keep cakes and biscuits. It wasn't really until the biscuit

McFarlane and Lang and Co. biscuit tin, 1837. (Emma Kay)

German biscuit tin, c. 1910.

factories and the mass production of baked goods soared in popularity towards the end of the nineteenth and beginning of the twentieth century, that high demand for bought goods led to the emergence of the cake and biscuit tin. Initially tins were manufactured as presentation boxes for the products themselves, but they were often so decorative that people kept them to use to store other items. Tin was followed by enamelware and then by glass, wood and aluminium tins, in a variety of shapes, sizes and patterns.

In addition to sweet biscuits, the early 1800s witnessed the growth of the savoury cracker. Jonathan Dodgson Carr, a Quaker and grocer's son, founded Carr's Biscuits in Carlisle around 1830, which soon became the largest mill and baking business in the country. Margaret Ann Brown worked in the factory in 1876, packing cream crackers and standing in a long line of twenty other women at a trestle table filling tin boxes full of straw with the biscuits. The factory walls were whitewashed to enhance the light, as the room was windowless except for a skylight. The women wore long white aprons, with their hair tied back. Biscuits were packed in four different sizes of tin, which were soldered and dispatched by rail, and then sea, across Europe. They even reached as far as Kenya, with a two-pound tin costing six shillings. A great imported luxury then.[9] By the middle of the twentieth century, Carr's, having remained a family business, was eventually procured by McVities and then United Biscuits.

Miscellaneous Storage

Bread and grain bins were called 'arks' and resembled large chests in the Middle Ages. They were particularly popular in the sixteenth century. By the 1800s earthenware 'bread crocks' emerged, eventually to be replaced the following century by the iconic enamel bread bin. I read somewhere once that in excess of ninety people a year injure themselves on bread bins in the UK. Whether this is true or not, I would really like to find out how a person can sustain any injuries from such a seemingly innocuous object.

Butter and fish were kept in standard 'firkins' – wooden or stoneware barrels – and meat was salted and hung from 'Dutch crowns', which were large iron hoops hooked to the ceiling.

Buckets have been numerous throughout history, with one for almost every function. In the finer households, buckets would have been made of mahogany and bound in brass. Some of the more distinctive designs include plate pails, which had an open side to enable plates to be slid in and out for careful transportation. Wine coolers often had

Preserved foods in jars, *c.* 1918.

pineapple finials, denoting both wealth and hospitality, whereas the shallow and wide oyster bucket stood on its four-legged frame, similar to the keeler, which was a bucket used in the dairy to hold milk, allowing it to settle so it would be easier to skim away the cream.[10]

Finally, the process of canning has a long and complicated history, the invention of which can be attributed to both the French and British. More can be found about this interesting story in *Dining with The Georgians*. However, the emergence of the screw-top jar was an even closer race for fame. Yorkshire born John Kilner invented a jar with a three-part lid consisting of a glass stopper, a rubber ring and a screw on metal collar and lid. Kilner was manufacturing glass jars in 1842, although the patented screw-top Kilner jar did not appear until the end of the nineteenth century. Simultaneously the American inventor and tinsmith John Landis Mason introduced his own screw-top jar around 1858. Yes, they of the much-coveted Mason and Kilner jars into which we hermetically seal our homemade jams, chutneys and sloe gin concoctions every year. It would take a further ten years for Mason to file his patent, allegedly because he was suspected of selling his jars prior to the two-year period stipulated by the patent submission. So exactly who invented the design first remains contentious. Incidentally, the controversial television broadcaster Jeremy Clarkson is the great-great-great grandson of John Kilner.[11]

The following instructions provide three alternatives for preserving fruit in 1866. Clearly this was a household not yet familiar with screw-top or Kilner technology. The suggested inclusion of alum was common, even endorsed by Isabella Beeton, to improve the longevity of preserves. By the late 1800s, sodium sulphite was also a common addition to the process. By 1925 the Public Health Preservation in Food Act compiled a comprehensive list of both prohibited and suitable substances to be used in preserving, which thankfully curtailed the use of strange and dangerous additives, as well as cleaning up the problem of shonky food street traders.

Fruit to Bottle

No 1 – Take any quantity of fruit you intend to preserve, pick it, and fill your bottles or jars, then fill the copper or pan with cold water, and set the bottles in up to the neck; then warm the water to the heat of 150° by the thermometer, let them stand in it for twenty minutes at this heat, and be careful the water does not vary. Have some boiling water ready to fill up the bottles with when they come out of the copper; fill them within 1 in. of the top, and let them be corked and waxed immediately. It is important that this be well done. All fruits are best not too ripe.

No 2 – Pick the stalks from the fruit, and put it into common black bottles. Cork down tightly, and put the bottles into a bread oven two hours or so after the bread has been drawn, and let them stay for several hours, so that the fruit may be very gradually done. After baking in this way the fruit will keep a year or two.

No 3 – Pick the stalks from the fruit and put them into bottles Put 1 dr of alum into 4 gallons of boiling water; let it stand until cold then; fill the bottles, bung them tight, then put them into a copper of cold water, and heat it to 176°. Then tie them over with bladder, and seal or resin them. On no account exceed the quantity of alum.[12]

2

Food Preparation

Every kitchen should have a big chopping board – I'm talking 3ft by 2ft.
Marco Pierre White
The Independent, 30 December 2012

Marco Pierre White could almost be referring to the nineteenth century in this quotation, when chopping blocks would easily be as large as half a tree trunk and always positioned as close to the kitchen table as possible. There is a curious story in the newspapers of 1868 – during a missing person's investigation; a house that police were searching as part of the investigation revealed a rather curious twist in proceedings. A large chopping board was discovered in the kitchen, welded to the floor. By accident, one of the officers touched a spring on the board, which, when released, exposed its hollow underside, and a tunnel leading directly into the London sewers below.[1] Well, I couldn't just leave the mystery there, could I? After a little further research into the case, I discovered that the missing person, Mr Speke, was caught trying to escape to America. On his journey to the docks in Liverpool, where he was to embark for America, he was persuaded by friends to return home and relieve the agony of his tortured family. This he reluctantly did, stating that he was overcome by some sort of temporary mania. The case dominated the press for some weeks with speculation and all sorts of rumours about the man himself and his fate. It emerged that the real reason Mr Speke had wanted to leave the country was to seek solitude and to preach the Gospel in a country where nobody knew anything about him. Whether he eventually got there or not was not revealed but I like to think he did. A curious, if rather sad case with a vague link to kitchenalia and one of many similar connections that you will encounter throughout this book.

Some of the most primitive, yet timeless items designed for the kitchen can be found in this chapter: implements that offer crude and basic functions – hitting, mashing, cutting, removing, weighing and measuring. One of the earliest of these is the pestle and mortar, used by the Babylonians from 2,500 BC or even earlier. A couple of rocks, or a rock and a wooden slab would have served as the initial version. The pestle and mortar doubled as the apothecaries' tool during the medieval period, right through to the eighteenth century, before finding a permanent home in every domestic kitchen as the best tool to grind, pulp and mince. It was particularly handy at breaking down the wealth of exotic new herbs, spices and of course sugar reaching British shores in the days when naval exploration, the import market and two-way migration boomed.

Chopping, Mincing, Grinding and Grating

Cast-iron gears emerged in the mid-nineteenth century and the race began to develop the most advanced parer – a convenient device to peel, trim, core and cut fruit – in particular apples, which were such a popular and abundant fruit in both America and Britain. America pipped Britain to the post (pardon the pun) because the development of this first mass-market kitchen aid was made in 1803, by Moses Coates. Once the technology was established, the basic fundamentals of the apple parer swiftly led to the invention of a whole host of useful cutting objects, such as the bean slicer, asparagus buncher and cutter, marmalade slicer and many more. Some have stood the test of time but many didn't, or were replaced by more sophisticated versions. By the late 1880s and early 1900s, the market was flooded with food grinders and choppers. Meat grinders became a kitchen staple by the end of the nineteenth century and would double-up as cheese graters. In fact, most meat grinders were used for fruit and nuts and other hard to break down foods while marmalade cutters, designed to shred oranges, had the more general purpose of slicing potatoes, carrots and other vegetables. Marmalade cutters were still widely used in kitchens well into the 1950s and there are advertisements for electric marmalade cutters as early as 1905.[2] Electric meat choppers were in circulation as early as 1913 and by the beginning of the 1930s, the American market was confidently promoting meat choppers combined with can openers and knife sharpeners together in one tidy unit.

Although archaeological finds determine that the Greeks were probably using bronze graters circa 1194 BC, like so many of our modern-day appliances, it was undoubtedly

Wooden nutmeg grater, *c.* 1830. (Emma Kay)

Left: Spong & Co. Ltd bean slicer.
Top right: Mouli 'Parsmint' and Victorian steel herb chopper.
Bottom right: Edwardian marmalade cutter. (Emma Kay)

the Romans that introduced Britain to the cheese grater. Bronze and silver cheese graters have been unearthed in the tombs of the Roman elite, suggesting that hard cheese was a luxury item and a grater was an essential utensil for the aristocratic Roman.[3]

Possibly the most popular of all graters from the eighteenth century was the nutmeg grater. In their crudest form, they were simply sheets of tin or iron pierced with holes, others were mounted on boards, with a small drawer to collect the nutmeg filings. Often nutmeg graters came in small lidded boxes, or pocket treens, which could be carried around and conveniently used when out and about to sweeten cakes, puddings or milky drinks. It is said that Charles Dickens was often known to carry one such luxury item around with him. And at around £400 for pound of nutmeg in today's money, the spice was still very much a luxury item during the eighteen and nineteenth centuries.

By the Victorian period, the market was flooded with mincers, choppers, slicers and all manner of gadgets. According to the media of that time, the bean slicer was newly invented in the 1860s, with the Batkins model being one of the first to be patented; however, it is the Spong model that remains the most iconic. James Osborn Spong, originally from Northampton, was educated in London and then quickly became a very successful entrepreneur of Spong & Co., specialising in household utensils. At one point

Above left: Twentieth-century meat grinder. (Emma Kay)
Above right: Contemporary Mason Cash mixing bowl and wooden spoon. (Emma Kay)

the company was the biggest and the most successful of its kind, stocking the kitchens of the royal family and the rich and famous.

The French company Mouli created and manufactured some of the best chopping and mincing gadgets from the 1930s to the 1960s and they were also popular in British households. The Moulinette had three cutting discs, suitable for 'mincing and chopping fish, suet, vegetables and fruit, preparing paste for sandwiches, stuffing, small pieces of raw and cooked meat'.[4] The Parsmint of the 1930s was cleverly designed to specifically chop and shred parsley and mint. The Mouli grater's iconic design is still used today to grate small items such as garlic, nutmeg, nuts etc. These were fantastic labour-saving utensils that looked wonderful as a collection of essential items for the modern kitchen, with their elegant shapes and coloured handles. Today, you may recognise the brand better as Moulinex, founded by the inventor Jean Mantelet in 1932.

Eighteenth and nineteenth century choppers looked very different, but their style and shape remain popular in the modern professional kitchen – from the classic crescent-shaped blade with a wooden handle, to the oblong, spade-like chopper.

Mixing

Most mixing bowls were made of wood prior to the seventeenth century, until earthenware products were manufactured for their durability and waterproof qualities. These were in plain, neutral colours. Coloured bowls began to make an appearance by the end of the nineteenth century. Usually the maker's mark was omitted on mixing bowls, making it difficult to determine the age and quality of older bowls. Many early earthenware bowls tended to have weaknesses, as they weren't fired at temperatures as high as used for china, and therefore have not survived as well as later versions. One way of determining the origin of mixing bowls is by the 'grip stand', including both the raised pattern on the outside of the mixing bowl, the slightly overhanging rim and pronounced chiselled out support. These were all integrated into the design to enable the user to keep the bowl steady when mixing and are characteristic of the 1930s, 40s and 50s, produced most famously by companies such as Mason Cash & Co. and T. G. Green & Co. It is also possible to date most bowls that have a lip to help with pouring liquids, as Victorian or post-Victorian.[5] The start of Mason Cash can be dated to the early 1800s in Derbyshire, where the village of Church Gresley was known for its quality pottery. Tom Cash bought the village enterprise from a master potter known as 'Bossy' Mason in 1901 and the name Mason, Cash & Co. was born.[6] The village of Church Gresley was also home to T. G. Green (Thomas Goodwin Green) who established his company in 1864 and found fame during the 1920s–30s for their distinctive Cornish ware, with its bold and stylish blue and white stripes, and later yellow and white stripes. It was thought that the blue and white was reminiscent of Cornish waves, hence the name.

Mason Cash bought out T.G. Green in 2001 but the company was then purchased by the Tabletop Co., before all production in Derbyshire ceased and it was outsourced to Europe. Thankfully the Mason Cash and T. G. Green names continue under the leading global house ware supplier, Rayware and Charles Rickards, and Paul Burston respectively.

Although the good, reliable results of the sturdy hand mixing bowl are still an essential part of kitchen life today, inevitably progress and technology have provided us with the bright, shiny trademark of the ubiquitous electric mixer. In her book *Post-War Kitchen*, Marguerite Patten, the esteemed culinary dame of the twentieth century, reminisces about her early work demonstrating the new-fangled electric mixers and liquidisers of the 1950s, at Harrods in London, during her time working with the Ministry of Food Bureau. Each morning and afternoon, with a small team of colleagues, Marguerite demonstrated the machines to the public, offering help with using them and advising on suitable recipes. One of the recipes she would demonstrate was for ham and tomato pâté, which I have included here as it sounds so simple and reassuringly 1950s, and was a perfect choice for those early liquidisers.

Ham and Tomato Pâté

Skin, deseed and chop 3 medium tomatoes. Dice 5oz (150g) lean ham. Put half the ingredients with a little made mustard and a shake of pepper into the liquidiser goblet, place the lid in position, switch on and process until smooth. Carefully remove the puree and repeat with the remaining ingredients.[7]

Weighing and Measuring

From the 1700s the imperial system of weights included three main types – avoirdupois weight, Troy weight and apothecaries' weight. Each of these used the abbreviation 'lb' (from the Latin, Libra, a Roman unit of weight), also used for the monetary pound. Pounds in weight were divided into ounces, abbreviated as 'oz.'.

Food and drink products would also have been sold in accordance with their volume and there were a number of specialist terms for these, based on the containers in which they were stored, rather than the weight itself. For example, butter was weighed in firkins, while a 'caddy' of tea would nearly always weigh around one and a third pounds. The avoirdupois system was applied to large bulky items. The dram or drachm was the smallest, equivalent to one ounce. Fourteen pounds was equal to one stone. Four quarters was one hundredweight (cwt), while twenty hundredweights were equivalent to one ton. The Troy weight was abandoned in 1878, but it is still used today to weigh precious stones and metals. Troy units of measure were used to weigh grains, with twenty-four grains equivalent to one pennyweight, and twenty pennyweights making up an ounce. Finally, apothecaries' weight was a system that remained in use right up until 1978. It was based on the process of weighing out powders by apothecaries or pharmacists. Twenty grains were equal to one scruple, while three scruples were a dram, and eight drams equalled an ounce.

Liquids were measured as twenty minims being equivalent to one fluid scruple, three fluid scruples made up one drachm and eight drachms made one fluid ounce (fl. oz.), while five fluid ounces amounted to one gill. Four gills were equivalent to one pint. Two pints made up a quart, and four quarts made one gallon. Dry goods were measured in pecks and bushels.[8]

It is also very important to remember that most recipes until the early twentieth century relied on guess work, even if terms we are familiar with such as ounces, fluid ounces, pounds and pints, were used. The same applies to temperatures and cooking times. One of the first culinary experts and recipe writers to provide such detail in the recipe methodology was Eliza Acton, whose work preceded Isabella Beeton's book and was almost certainly plagiarised to an extent by her. Below is Eliza's recipe for Italian Pork Cheese, taken from the iconic *Modern Cookery for Private Families*. It is staggering the amount of detail she provides her readers with, which was revolutionary at this time.

Italian Pork Cheese

Chop, not very fine, one pound of lean pork with two pounds of the inside fat; strew over, and mix thoroughly with them three teaspoonful of salt, nearly half as much pepper, a half tablespoonful of mixed parsley, thyme and sage (and sweet basil if it can be procured), all minced extremely small. Press the meat closely and evenly into a shallow tin, – such as are used for Yorkshire puddings will answer well, – and bake it in a very gentle oven from an hour to an-hour-and-a-half: it is served cold in slices. Should the proportion of fat be considered too much, it can be diminished on a second trial. Minced mushrooms or truffles may be added with very good effect to all meat-cakes or compositions of this kind. Lean of pork, 1 lb; fat 2 lbs; salt, 3 teaspoonfuls; pepper, 1½ teaspoonful; mace, ½ teaspoonful, nutmeg 1 small; mixed herbs, 1 large tablespoonful: 1 to 1½ hour.[9]

The *Encyclopaedia of Domestic Economy* of 1855 recommends that 'a good balance or pair of scales is necessary. It is requisite to have scales for ordinary uses, and others for occasions when greater delicacy is required. Fine scales should be kept in a box secluded from the air, and should never be overloaded. They should be used in a good light'.[10]

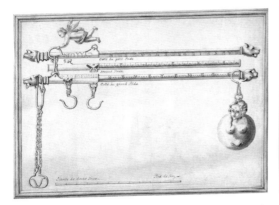 

Above left: Eighteenth-century weighing scales.
Above right: 1914 'spring balance' scales.

Self-indicating scales did not emerge until the nineteenth century, although Leonardo Da Vinci famously designed an early invention in the 1500s that was never developed. The beam scale is probably the most recognisable of scales, thought to have been developed around 1500 BC, although it's likely to have been earlier.

Counter-balance scales with a tin pan on one side and cast-iron weights of varying sizes the other are the most synonymous with Victorian weighing – in the kitchen and in retail establishments – and are sometimes still used today. Then spring-balance scales were introduced and the leading manufacturer, since the mid-1700s, has been Salter. However, Nicholl et al (1860) suggested that Salter's scales were not accurate, declaring them 'liable to vary with the temperature, and also to become relaxed by constant use;

Left: Street seller weighing cherries on a beam scale, 1759. (Paul Sandby, Yale)
Opposite: Peeling potatoes, c. 1880.

it has no weights or counterpoise belonging to it'.[11] W&T Avery were also one of the main British manufacturers of weighing machines, established around the same time as Salter's, also in the West Midlands. Both company names are still trading today but are owned by large global corporations. The well-known German company Krups was also a popular manufacturer of early twentieth century spring-balance scales, designed for the European market and made in bright art deco colours, making them a popular addition to the British kitchen in the 1920s.

Wooden mugs of varying sizes were commonly used to measure out ingredients in British kitchens during the 1700s. By the following century, pewter and earthenware measures were the popular choice, while tin measures were used for shellfish. As domestic weighing scales became more useful in the kitchen, measuring equipment was used for liquids only. Aluminium measuring ware was at the height of fashion in the early twentieth century, with the Swan brand dominating the market. Glass and enamel measuring receptacles were also widely used.[12] The Swan brand range of brushed aluminium domestic wares was endorsed by the nineteenth century brass founders Bulpitt & Sons. By the 1940s they were manufacturing special lines including chrome-plated and Carlton Ware products, in addition to new small electrical goods. The Tala graduated cook's measure for liquid and dried goods was one of the more typical, brightly-coloured and scored cone-shaped measuring utensils of the 1950s and has recently been re-vamped for the new retail market as part of the vintage Tala kitchen ware range.

3

Dairy

My antique butter churner. It makes me think about the days when things were done properly but not necessarily quickly. The rest of the team thought I'd gone mad when I turned up with what they saw as a piece of junk, but they've changed their tune now.
Nathan Outlaw, Restaurant Nathan Outlaw, Outlaw's Fish Kitchen, Port Isaac.
Outlaw's at the Capital Hotel, London. The Mariner's Rock, Rock.
The Guardian, 'I Couldn't Live Without … Top Chefs' Favourite Kitchen Kit', 2011

Cream, Cheese and Butter-Making Tools

There have been numerous types and sizes of churns, the wooden barrel being the oldest method, then there is the 'dasher' churn, the dasher being the stick that was plunged up-and-down, by hand, in an upright container made of either wood or earthenware. By the early twentieth century the glass churn with wooden beaters became a popular choice in the domestic kitchen, while eggbeaters and electric hand whisks proved to be useful alternatives. Paddles and ladles were also used for smaller quantities of butter, often worked in a bowl or small churn. As much of the older dairy equipment was woodenware, it had to be soaked in boiling water then immersed in cold water until it was ready to be used again.

In *Cattle, Sheep and Deer*, published in 1872, the suggested necessary dairy utensils are listed as: 'Churns, milk pails, hair sieves, slices of tin and wood, milk pans, marble dishes for cream, scales and weights, portable drying rack, wooden bowls, butter moulds, butter patters, wooden tubs for washing'.

There are a number of old wives tales relating to butter making. If a cow is only milked once a day she will only yield a small amount of butter, as opposed to milking twice a day. However, if milked three times in one day, there may be more milk available, but it will be of a less rich consistency. Milk a cow in the morning and the milk will be of a much higher quality than if milked in the evening.

It would also have been common practice in the mid-nineteenth century for just one woman to manage the cheese and butter-making of up to and maybe even beyond a herd of thirty cows.

The Farmer's Register of 1835 describes the process of making butter in Scotland in the late Georgian era. It lists the three components of milk as viz, lactose and whey. The oily viz

Top left: Churning butter in the early 1700s.
Above left: Carrying a milk pail, 1850.
Above right: Milkmaid with yoke.

is what is needed to make the butter, created in the churning and agitating process. When initially drawn from the cow, the milk is placed in coolers for up to twelve hours prior to churning. After the first few minutes of churning, hot water is added to allow the milk to reach above seventy degrees before the butter can be separated from the milk. The milk should then be churned for some two-and-a-quarter to two-and-three-quarters of an hour. Sugar and salt is then added to improve the overall taste. We are informed that sometimes the cream is skimmed off and churned or mixed with whey to make a better quality butter.[1]

The following is a recipe for Cheshire cheese production in 1850:

To make cheese all the whey needs to be extracted and the curd cured from the milk. The milk is left overnight and any cream is skimmed off. A proportion of the milk is then heated in a large pan, poured into a 'cheese tub' (similar to a brewing tub), and the remaining cold milk added. Rennet (generally the stomach of calves) is then added,

Left: 1930s square glass jar butter churn.
Top right: Late Georgian brass skimmer.
Bottom right: Victorian butter patters and butter wheel. (Emma Kay)

mixed with lukewarm water and salt, passed through a sieve. The milk mixture is stirred well, covered and then left to coagulate for an hour or so. The curd is removed either by hand, with a skimming dish or a curd-breaker (a kind of oval wire grill with a tin rim). The curd then separates and sinks to reveal the whey, which is extracted and placed in another pan. The curd which sinks to the bottom is pressed with a wooden board with holes to allow more whey to be eked out. And various other presses, replacing the even older tradition of a pole being pressed down onto the curd by hand. Once all of the whey has been removed, the curd is salted and crumbled, wrapped in 'cheese cloth' and then pressed again, this continues over several days whereby the cheese is pressed, skewered and turned to ensure it is thoroughly dried and free from whey. The cheese is removed from its vat, covered in a bandage or 'fillet', slated and placed on stone or wooden shelves, turned daily and applied with fresh salt and bandages. This process of drying and salting can take from seven to twenty days, depending on the season.[2]

Although most large country houses had their own dairy, farmers would deliver milk and cream to local homes; but by the late nineteenth century due to the growth in urban relocation, large commercial dairies like Express Dairies, established in 1864, grew in strength. It's heartening to see that this wasn't just a job for the boys as one advertisement for a Scottish creamy in 1917 was recruiting for a 'Dairy delivery foreman (or woman), [to] take charge [of] small depot, apply with references…'[3] However I appreciate this was during the First World War so men were in short supply.

Many people still made their own cream and butter at home right up until the 1950s, although cheese was always purchased from the grocer or at the market. The process of making butter is very simple, involving the agitation of cream until it thickens, shaped using wooden butter pats dipped in warm salted water to prevent the butter sticking. Butter ballers and curlers became popular tools to form the butter into attractive shapes. Butter was also stamped both for aesthetics and to denote which dairy it came from, particularly as it was common for dairy farmers or their wives to take surplus butter to sell at markets. A distinguishing trademark was required to ensure people were aware of the farm of origin. Urban dairies disappeared by the 1920s with the expansion of rail. This enabled rural farmers to transport their churns of milk by rail, which was then distributed to homes. Initially, billycans – miniature churns – would be left on doorsteps; glass milk bottles, sealed with wax discs, were not in widespread use until the beginning of the twentieth century. They were also popular in picnic sets, along with plates, cups, sandwich tins, flasks and aluminium jars in the 1930s.

Dairies could be dangerous places and the press contain quite a number of stories relating to incidents that took place in these butter and cheese making rooms. In Stonehouse in 1922 a two-year-old girl fell into a hot milk pan in her father's dairy. She was so severely scalded that she died a couple of days after the accident.[4] A four-year-old child fell into a churning machine in Nevins in 1921 and died from her injuries, which included two broken arms and two broken legs.[5] In 1893 a modernised dairy, fitted with some of the latest equipment, took the life of a young twenty-two-year-old woman who, whilst engaged in cleaning down some of the machinery, got her hair caught in the mechanisms, tearing her scalp off completely from the nape of her neck to her eyebrows.[6] Another young woman working in a dairy in Co. Antrim in 1939 got her clothing caught

Below left: Victorian butter wheel.
Below right: Edwardian butter knives.
Bottom right: Twentieth-century cheese dish and butter knife. (Emma Kay)

up in the machinery, and the clothes twisted round her neck and strangled her.[7] The sanitary conditions of dairies also came into question in 1889 when typhoid fever swept across Leeds as a consequence of milk supplied by a farm who had employed someone with the disease who then contaminated the milk during production.[8] It would make an interesting study to research the levels of accidents and deaths in dairies prior to the industrial revolution when only basic hand-held tools were required.

Manufacturers became pre-occupied with inventing improved domestic dairy tools for the housewives of the 1950s – from whistling milk pans to combined hand-held beaters and whisks. After the bleak wartime years, there was a great boom in butter, cream and milk consumption as well as all associated products. This was a consequence of restrictions placed on dairy farmers, and the illegal sale of cream. In fact, real cream did not become available in Britain again until 1953. For some children and young people born between the late 1930s–50s, all they had known was evaporated milk or worse still, 'Mock Cream', a recipe for which Marguerite Patten included in her 1998 edition of *Post-War Kitchen*.

Mock Cream

Cream 1oz (25g) butter or margarine (it is worthwhile using butter if you can spare it) with 1/2 -1oz (15-25g) caster or sifted icing sugar.

Very gradually beat teaspoons of the cornflour mixture into the creamed fat and sugar.

An electric mixer does this very efficiently but whether mixing by hand or by machine, the secret is to incorporate the cornflour mixture slowly and beat hard.

For a less thick cream, follow the method given but use 4oz (115g) butter to the 71/2 fl oz (225 ml) milk.[9]

Below left: Churning butter, 1799.
Below right: Girl eating ice cream, 1913.

As Marguerite points out, the strict rationing also meant that butter was frequently substituted by margarine. Silver Seal margarine was one of the top wartime brands, retailing at just 9d a *1b* in 1940.[10] The quality of margarine generally was poor, made from low-grade materials. It may even had been as bad as when the first Margarine Act was passed in 1887, forcing all manufacturers of margarine to register with local authorities who had the powers to test their products at any time. This was largely in response to research published by the medical journal, *The Lancet,* which exposed the high levels of adulteration, thought to have dire consequences on public health, if continued.[11] Often during the Second World War, margarine was added to butter, and marketed as a pure butter product.

Ice-Cream Making Tools

Another dairy product that suffered from the addition of low-grade margarine during the Second World War, was ice-cream.

King Charles II was supposed to be the first person ever to eat an ice-cream made on British soil, in 1671, following the European fashion for all things *acque gelate.* Originally, simple ice-creams were made in lidded pewter pots from ice, milk and eggs and stored in ice houses.

Then elaborate moulds – with intricate carved patterns, from flowers to birds – were used as centre pieces in the dining rooms of large country estates, while Italian migrants settling in Britain during the 1800s fuelled the fire for exotic new flavours and techniques. This had evolved into a large-scale industry by the end of the nineteenth century with vendors on almost every street corner and manufacturers retailing ice-cream in shops, restaurants, cafes and hotels throughout Britain. Perhaps one of the most famous ice-cream makers of all to trade in Britain was Carlo Gatti, whose 'HokeyPokey' ice-cream slabs of the mid-1800s, wrapped in paper and served as 'penny licks' became a phenomenally popular street snack.[12]

The wider ice-cream industry – unlike the product itself – was not all sweetness and light. The HokeyPokey came in for criticism amongst some religious groups, such as the Methodist Church, which in 1924, called for restrictions regarding Sunday trading of the HokeyPokey. This was due to the fact that a number of children had been found spending their pennies on this much coveted ice-cream, rather than adding it to the Sunday School collection box.[13] As often seems to be the case, many street vendors tried to replicate the popular HokeyPokey trademark ice-cream, and the substitute versions were frequently reported to be made out of adulterated products, like the ones found to be made of mashed swede and turnip being sold on the streets of Manchester in 1881.[14]

The disputes, fights and deaths amongst Italian ice-cream vendors in Britain during the nineteenth and early twentieth century were very serious and numerous. Some were just internal gang turf wars and family-related disagreements, while others were crimes related to prejudice and persecution of Italians as a race, fuelled by disgruntled British nationals who resented their success. The press was flooded with these types of stories throughout this period. More can be found about this interesting area of cultural culinary history in *Dining with the Victorians.*

Another ice-cream pioneer, Agnes Marshall, was quite possibly one of the fiercest, most ambitious and successful women of her generation, not just in the field of culinary arts, but also as an astute, intelligent, forward-thinking individual. Yet she remains annoyingly elusive and under-researched. One reason for this is that a great deal of material about her and her work was destroyed in a fire. She also only lived a short life. Her list of credits includes:

- Writing two fundamental books on ices that both popularised the product amongst the middle classes during the nineteenth century and provide an inspirational account of some of the period's long lost recipes and ideas for working with iced treats.
- The undoubted inventor, advocate and national promoter of one of the first ice-cream making machines
- Potentially the first person to add ice-cream/sorbet to a cone
- The instigator for using liquefied gas in the manufacture of ice-cream
- Establishing the highly successful Marshall School of Cookery in 1883.[15]

Here is a sample of some of the reviews that Marshall's School of Cookery received from the press, which appear in Agnes's *Book of Ices* "Excellent classes." – *Leicester Post*, "Genius for good cooking", *Northampton Guardian*, "Unanimous praise." – *Bedford Recorder*, "A school of elegance and fashion." – *National Philanthropist* and so on. The school was one of the best in the world, if not *the* best and had a turnover of thousands of students each year attending either one day, or three, six and twelve month courses.

Below is Agnes's recipe for iced coffee soufflé:

Take a soufflé dish and surround it inside with paper standing about 2 inches above the top, and put it into the charged cave to get cold.

Take and whip over boiling water 12 raw yolks of eggs, 6 whites, 4 large tablespoonfuls of very strong coffee, 4 ounces of castor sugar, until like a thick batter, then remove and continue the whipping on ice till the mixture is cold; to this quantity add 2 teacupfuls of whipped cream; pour this into the mould, letting it rise above the mould to near the top of the paper. Freeze in the cave for 2½ hours, and serve in the mould with napkin round or in silver soufflé dish.[16]

Marshall's Patent Freezer was being advertised as early as 1885, boasting the creation of the finest ices in just three to five minutes, with no ice packing or spatulas required. Essentially it was a shallow drum that was turned by hand. An example of one of Mrs Marshall's incredible early gadgets can be seen at the London Canal Museum. The 'cave' that she refers to in the above recipe was another of her inventions for storing the ice-cream, once it was prepared.

4

Drinks

My Homer Simpson bottle-opener, a present from my PA, Zabrina.
Each time I open a bottle, it goes, 'Mmmmmmm, beer.'
Tom Kerridge, The Hand & Flowers, Marlow, Buckinghamshire
The Guardian, 'I Couldn't Live Without … Top Chefs' Favourite Kitchen Kit', 2011

Tea Caddies and Tea Accessories

As a consequence of unfiltered and therefore unsanitary water, for centuries Britain invested in brewing and drinking a wide variety of beverages, ranging from Medieval ales, meads, and ciders; to hot drinks like tea, coffee and chocolate; the Georgian age's hard liquor, such as gut-rotting gins; to Victorian carbonated waters and cordials, and the Edwardians' preference, American cocktails. All these drinks come with their own set of

Above left: Drinking from a tankard in the 1800s.
Above right: Morning tea, 1758.

infusing and brewing equipment, as well as receptacles with which to serve them and from which to drink them.

The first official consignment of tea came to Britain in the mid-1600s. Initially it was an expensive commodity and highly taxed, but craved by the wealthy and aspiring middle classes. It was drunk by women at home, and by men in some of the more salubrious coffee houses that crowded the streets at this time. The push and pull of demand and high prices resulted in smuggling and black market activities. Tea, like many other staple goods at the time, also became adulterated to make it cheaper. By the eighteenth century, the heavy duties were lifted and the drink became a widespread, popular beverage with the masses, along with the demand for receptacles to serve it, store it in, and drink it out of.

This was the time of the big factories and potteries. Men like Spode and Wedgwood were busy producing the wonderful 'china' services – so called after the delicate blue and white imports from China.

The word caddy is derived from the Malaysian 'kati' which was an old unit of weight for measuring tea. It is understood that the oldest caddy dates to around 1708, made by the silversmith Thomas Ash. By the time that George I took the throne, silver caddies were a popular item. Early designs were usually a straight-sided container, shaped a bit like a bottle, with shoulders and a narrow neck with a pull-off cap. They were initially very plain, with the only decoration likely to be a featured cap of some sort.[1]

Many early tea caddies were made with locks as a consequence of tea's early relationship with theft and adulteration. And some caddies had several compartments for the varieties of black and green tea entering the British market.

'Tea balls' and 'tea eggs' were just some of the labels applied to tea infusers during the nineteenth century. Filled with loose tea and immersed in a cup or pot of hot water, tea

Georgian tea caddy, spoon and sugar nipper.

infusers could be very elaborate, crafted in silver with filigree patterns. Tea bags were not conceived until 1908 when Thomas Sullivan, an American tea merchant, decided to place samples of his tea in little silk bags tied with string as a useful marketing gimmick for his customers. Even then it wasn't until the 1940s that the tea bag design became more sophisticated and suitable for the mass market. Originally flat, square or rectangular, tea bags are now fashioned in all sorts of ways, including pyramids and circles, complete with the option of an individual one-cup sterving.[2] The earliest known teaspoon – that is a spoon specifically designed to stir tea – is known to be from around 1670 and made of unmarked silver. The earliest teakettle reportedly resides in the collections of Norwich Castle Museum, dating to circa 1694. Early silver 'kettles' were placed on a stand, with a spirit burner to provide enough heat to brew the tea.

The acclaimed Sally Lunn tea and eating house, in Bath, boasts a culinary heritage dating back to the fifteenth century and beyond. It is also home of the unique Sally Lunn bun, the creation of one of Bath's most famous Huguenot baking refugees, Solange Luyon. Considered one of the best accompaniments to tea, the following recipe proudly proclaims that 'once eaten at your table, [it] will cause your friends to rejoice when asked to come again'.

> Take a stone pot, pour in one-pint bowl of sweet milk, half a teacup bakers' or other yeast, one quarter of a pound of melted butter, a little salt, and three beaten eggs. Mix in three-pint bowls of flour; let it stand several hours, until quite light, then put it into Turk-heads or other tin pans, in which Sally should again rise before shoved into the oven, to be "brought out" and presented to your friends as the beauty and belle of the evening.[3]

Victorian copper kettle. (Emma Kay)

Coffee Mills and Percolators

The way in which we consume coffee in the UK home today has a long and interesting narrative that is surprisingly more British than might be at first be thought. From fireplace to cafetière, the British contribution to coffee making and grinding apparatus is worthy of comparison with that of the French and the Italians. Coffee was first imported to Britain in 1660. By 1801, total consumption of coffee from the US to Britain reached 980,141lb. Just seventy years later this had escalated to a staggering 40,000,000lb.[4]

Most coffee beans were roasted at home in a big old iron drum over the fire and then they had to be ground down laboriously using a pestle and mortar. It is understood that Nicholas Brook invented the first coffee mill in 1657 and could be bought at the 'Frying Pan' in Tooley Street, London, for around two old pounds. That's around £200 today.[5]

The first definitive references to hand-operated coffee mills in British newspapers start to appear around 1736. References to coffee mills in personal family papers are

Left: A Red Cross van, serving coffee and doughnuts to US military, *c.* 1943.
Below: Edwardian coffee pot, Georgian papier mâché tray and 1940s coffee mill. (Emma Kay).

also evident in Britain from 1712. As the price of coffee came down, the mills and grinders became less of a luxury and more of an essential piece of equipment. According to one Lancashire factory, in 1832 it was manufacturing an average of 90,000 new domestic wooden coffee mills a year.[6] In addition to Lancashire being recognised as an area associated with coffee mill makers, Wolverhampton is also considered to be of significance in this area of manufacture. A search of the Trade Directories throughout the 1800s, by county, suggests the main manufacturing regions were London, the West and East Midlands, Lancashire, and a few located in Wiltshire. It is assumed that this was due to the presence of so many iron and brass foundries in these regions, the materials earliest coffee mills were cast in. The impact of the heightened popularity of coffee drinking in coffee houses undoubtedly hit the traditional coffee mill maker hardest. According to the census, by 1901 there are just twenty-one coffee mill makers operating in Wolverhampton and after 1910 it is difficult to find reference to any coffee mill makers, suggesting that the consumption of coffee mills was already in decline.

Coffee percolators start to make an appearance as retail items in the British press from the beginning of the nineteenth century. It was an Englishman, George Biggin who invented the first percolator as early as the 1780s and this is when the filtered coffee movement began to emerge. Incidentally, Biggin was one of the party of people to participate in the first balloon flight in Britain in 1785. The concept of percolating coffee using coffee in a bag, often made of cheesecloth or muslin that was dipped in a pot or cup, similar to our teabags of today, was being explored in a variety of ways during the 1800s. A British patent was filed in 1899 for filtration bags distributed from 'coin-freed machines' to allow one cup of instant coffee to be produced. The idea that a coffee vending machine could have been available as early as 1899 is extraordinary.

The Etzensberger Patent Cafetière was in circulation by 1880 and Etzensberger received a British Patent for his 'improvements in apparatus for making infusions extracts from substances by steam pressure' in 1878.[7] Born in Zurich, Etzensberger took up permanent residence in the U.K. and became the manager of the now recently-revamped Midland Grand Hotel in St Pancras. The well-known holiday travel entrepreneur Thomas Cook collaborated with *Etzensberger* when designing the appearance and layout of his international hotels and we are informed that:

> Although the apparatus has been for many weeks in full and successful operation in Mr. Cook's boarding-house for English tourists, in the Rue de la Faisanderie, Avenue du Bois de Boulogne, they look askance on an invention calculated to supersede their traditional and costly process of coffee-making.[8]

Chocolate

Another type of mill that was born in the Georgian era and remained popular into the 1900s was the chocolate mill. A small Molinillo, or chocolate agitator, was placed in the centre of a pot, similar to a coffee pot, and, as Cassell's Dictionary of Cookery, 1892. Explains one had to:

> ...mix the chocolate smoothly, with the water or milk and pour it into the pot; put on the lid with the handle of the mill coming through it and then warm the chocolate

gently, rubbing the handle briskly between the palms of the hands, all of the time the chocolate is on fire.

It is reinforced that the chocolate mustn't be allowed to boil, on account that it becomes 'oily'. Rather it should be in a 'fine state of froth' when the lid is finally removed.

This is a hot chocolate recipe that was published by Eliza Acton, a peer of Isabella Beeton. Taken from her famous book *Modern Cookery for Private Families*, in 1845, Acton listed ingredients and suggested cooking times, rather than saying things like 'when it is crusty round the edges' or other rather unhelpful basic instructions that many old recipe books provided.

TO MAKE CHOCOLATE.

An ounce of chocolate, if good, will be sufficient for one person. Rasp, and then boil it from five to ten minutes with about four tablespoonsful of water; when it is extremely smooth add nearly a pint of new milk, give it another boil, stir it well, or mill it, and serve it directly. For water-chocolate use three-quarters of a pint of water instead of the milk, and send rich hot cream to table with it. The taste must decide whether it shall be made thicker or thinner.

Chocolate, 2 oz.; water, quarter-pint, or rather more; milk, 1¼ : ½ minute.

Obs.—The general reader will understand the use of the chocolate-mill shown in the engraving with the pot; but to the uninitiated it may be as well to observe, that it is worked quickly round between both hands to give a fine froth to the chocolate. It also serves in lieu of a whisk for working creams, or jellies, to a froth or *whip*.

Papier Mâché Tray

By the late Georgian period it was important to display all of the lovely new china ware that the likes of Wedgwood and Spode were producing in their thriving Stoke factories. The eighteenth century saw the introduction of papier mâché, which was a less expensive rival to wooden items. Papier mâché was invented in China in the second century. By the middle of the nineteenth century, more than thirty companies in England were producing everything from letter openers to entire bedroom suites in papier mâché. The advent of the Arts and Crafts movement saw the rise in popularity of simplicity and the less ornate, making the manufacturing of papier mâché redundant by the end of the First World War.

Undoubtedly the tea tray and all its accompaniments would have become even more in demand at a time when the first reference to afternoon tea was also recorded, in the Georgian period. The Duchess of Bedford would complain about a slump in her energy levels around four o'clock and began requesting a tray containing tea, bread and butter, and cake, in order to counteract this. The fashion caught on as her society friends emulated her.[9] The Duchess of Bedford, or Anna Russell, lived until she was about seventy-four, which was quite an age in that era of high mortality. Perhaps it was all those afternoon teas that prolonged her life.

Edwardian silver plated chocolate pot, twentieth century Molinillo, nineteenth century blue and white china ware. (Emma Kay)

Other Drinks

Non-alcoholic drinks were phenomenally popular during the eighteenth and nineteenth centuries. One reason was they were promoted by the rampantly active Temperance Society to counter the evil, ugly repercussions of gin and home brewing. Secondly, chocolate and many new exotic teas and coffees were being imported and became available in the coffee houses, teashops and grocers. Then there were soft drinks in the form of fizzy water. Johann Schweppe discovered how to carbonate mineral water and this enabled him to introduce his pioneering business to London in the late 1700s, making bottled water for the masses. The most popular of these bottles was known as a

Schweppes & Co. Ltd's 'torpedo' bottle, an early carbonate mineral water container. (Emma Kay)

Torpedo, developed in the early to mid-1800s at his factory in Oxford Street, London. The bottle had to be laid flat to keep the cork wet and the carbonation in.

Imported French red wine was rapidly becoming the drink of the middle classes as well as the wealthy. It was more accessible and frequently used in cooking. In the city of Chester alone there were thirteen wine and spirit retailers in 1781, that number almost doubled to twenty-five by 1834.[10] By 1798, the invention of lithography and improvements in printing meant it was possible to print wine labels in large quantities. Prior to this, labels were hand written and tied to the neck of the bottle.

One drink that continues through time, changing and adapting to the seasons and various ingredients, is punch. Early punch bowls were made of silver, and later ceramics, and would often come with a variety of accessories such as ladles and special punch cups. Punch originated in India and migrated from there to England in the 1600s. Punch means 'five' in Hindi and therefore punch should traditionally be a mix of five alcoholic or non-alcoholic

Naval officers making punch.

Assortment of drinking glasses, 1871.

drinks. Originally these five ingredients were alcohol, sugar, lemon, water, and tea or spices. However, it may not always have been as many as five as in an old book of travels, dated 1639, a certain drink is mentioned called palepuntz, used by the English at Surat, (a city in Gujarat) composed of brandy, rosewater, citron-juice, and sugar. Eventually punch became a popular drink throughout Europe and America and is particularly synonymous with Christmas. This is an extract from Charles Dickens' novel *A Christmas Carol*:

> 'A merry Christmas, Bob!' said Scrooge, with an earnestness that could not be mistaken, as he clapped him on the back. 'A merrier Christmas, Bob, my good fellow, than I have given you, for many a year! I'll raise your salary, and endeavour to assist your struggling family, and we will discuss your affairs this very afternoon, over a Christmas bowl of smoking bishop, Bob!'[11]

The 'bishop' that Dickens refers to here is a derivative of punch and one of the oldest winter beverages, mainly composed of oranges, sugar and wine. It was the popular drink in the early universities in England, particularly Oxford.

Of equal antiquity, and of nearly the same composition as punch is the wassail bowl, which in many parts of England is still partaken of on Christmas Eve, and is alluded to by Shakespeare in his play, *A Midsummer Night's Dream*. In Jesus College, Oxford, we are told, it is drunk on the Festival of St David, out of a silver gilt bowl holding ten gallons, which was presented to the College by Sir Watkin William Wynne, in 1732. Here is an early recipe, for this most festive of drinks:

> Put into a quart of warm beer one pound of raw sugar,
> on which grate a nutmeg and some ginger;
> then add four glasses of sherry and two quarts more of beer,
> with three slices of lemon;
> add more sugar, if required,
> and serve it with three slices of toasted bread floating in it.[12]

In George Roberts' *Cups and Customs* of 1869, he recounts a punch recipe of one Billy Dawson. Roberts also reiterates that when mixing drinks, it is essential to 'let your utensils be clean, and your ingredients of first-rate quality':

> Sugar, twelve tolerable lumps;
> hot water, one pint;
> lemons, two, the juice and peel;
> old Jamaica rum, two gills;
> brandy, one gill;
> porter or stout, half a gill;
> arrack, a slight dash.
> I allow myself five minutes to make a bowl on the foregoing proportions, carefully stirring the mixture as I furnish the ingredients until it actually foams; and then: Kangaroos! how beautiful it is !!'[13]

5

Cookware

We acquired an Aga when we moved to the country. The dog and grandchildren love it, and it tempts me to cook. I have four ovens – for roasting, simmering, baking and warming. The roasting oven has bottom heat, so you can put things like flans in it without baking blind. I was asked to write *The Aga Book* in 1994 and it's still in print. I'm called the Aga Queen or some such rubbish.

Mary Berry, culinary icon
The Telegraph, 4 Nov. 2011

Above: Note the hearth on the left of this 1762 picture.
Left: Spit roasting during the same year would have looked something like this.

Ovens

Early cooking took place around a crude basic hearth – a fireplace with a fireback, which protected the masonry at the bottom of the chimney, and an open grate, which controlled the heat. Pots and kettles could be raised and lowered, suspended by a hook and chain from swinging iron bars. Most pots had tripod feet to allow them to stand directly in the embers of the fire. A bread oven was often built into the wall next to the fireplace. From the seventeenth century onwards, cloam ovens were particular to Devon and Cornwall; they were built from clay and were put into the chimneybreast itself. The raised hearth was a slightly later invention, with a low oven built into the structure of the hearth itself. The tabletop stove emerged during the eighteenth century. This was basically a brick-built stove with a cast-iron top to heat pots and pans. By the early nineteenth century, the cast-iron range became the popular choice in wealthier households. Early designs featured a closed oven to the side, with a basket grate as the main cooking device; the spit-turning issues of the century before were tackled with the addition of a handle that turned a spur gear, which in turn moved a rack and altered the position of the fire plate. Thomas Robinson's 1780 open range also integrated a tank for hot water. As industrialisation progressed, the open range was swiftly replaced by the closed range, patented in 1802. This essentially meant that the chimney was blocked in order to divert the heat directly into the ovens using a series of flues.

Kitchen and impressive hearth, *c.* 1820s

Kitchen interior, Plymouth Hoe, 1859.

Sir Benjamin Thompson, Count Rumford, was fundamental to the next stage of kitchen range development. An Anglo-American physicist and inventor of the Georgian age, who you can read a great deal more about in *Dining with The Georgians,* was developing technology to both conserve fuel and enhance the cooking process ahead of many other innovators in the field. It would be his early roaster, a self-contained unit that sat flush with the front of the range brickwork, heated via flues, that heralded the closed 'kitcheners' of the mid- to late nineteenth century. This iconic design then evolved into the typical oven design that we are all familiar with today. The first gas stoves were developed in the 1820s and there was a widespread campaign nationally to demonstrate both the cookers themselves and how to cook with them, as illustrated in this 1840 article from the *Leicester Journal*:

On Tuesday week, Mr. James Sharp of Winchester, delivered a lecture at Uppingham, on the application of gas to culinary and other purposes, during which several joints of meat, fowls, fish &c., were cooked. The dinner so cooked was afterwards served up to a large and respectable party of ladies and gentlemen, comprising shareholders in the Gas Company, town inspectors and other friends. The gas cookery was admired, and the entertainment much enhanced by the presence of the ladies, which had an effect at once novel and agreeable.[1]

By the Edwardian era, kitchen fixtures and fittings were made to be practical and simple, sinks were lined with zinc or stone, and tiles were very popular. The kitchener was a closed-top range, with a hot plate made of cast iron, and by the early twentieth century was the range of choice in most kitchens that could afford it. Some stood independently on four legs and usually ran on gas. By this time, oil and electricity were alternative fuels but still expensive ones. The inter-war years marked a turning point with the

Above: A 1930s US kitchen.
Right: The Aga inventor, Gustaf
Dalén, 1900.

introduction and sale of electric cookers, from just five thousand in 1923, to one-and-a-half-million by 1939. This can largely be attributed to early difficulties with adapting to new techniques in cooking, as well as the cost, both of the oven itself, and the amount of energy it consumed.[2]

It was in 1922 that blind Nobel Prize-winning physicist Dr Gustaf Dalén invented the world's first heat-storage cooker. The AGA. Confined to his home after a failed experiment cost him his sight, Dalén was inspired to create a better, more efficient cooker for his wife, Elma, who constantly had to tend to their old-fashioned range.

Dalén created a cast-iron cooker capable of every kind of cooking simultaneously, through its two large hotplates and two ovens.

Cooking ranges in the 1930s were often finished in smart enamel and may have included a boiler for hot water in the kitchen and glass windows to view cooking. All modern builds came with gas or electricity supplies, and aluminium ware was favoured for the electric hob. Cupboards began to be built-in and fitted to keep the dust out and create more storage space.

Cooking Apparatus

Abraham Darby, the first in a long line of iron manufacturers, started his business at a time when cast-iron pots were the staple of working class cooking. During the early 1700s in Britain the process of casting was very limited and as a consequence these types of pots were mostly imported from abroad. Darby cast his pots in sand and founded the famous Coalbrookedale furnace, manufacturing and selling good quality cast iron pots to the nation.

Gridiron

The best way to picture the gridiron is to think of the grill you have on your barbeque. In open fire cooking, it was the grill that was placed directly over the fire. In 1913 an article appeared in the *Sevenoaks Chronicle and Kentish Advertiser*, describing how best to care for your gridiron:

> If possible use one of steel with slender bars; the common broad, flat iron bars fry and scorch the meat. Each time before using, grease it with fresh, sweet suet, and wipe with paper; after using see that it is scrupulously clean before putting away.

This 1833 cartoon features a good image of a gridiron.

Far from being a boring ordinary everyday object, there is a rather grisly account recorded in the 'News from Ireland' section of the November 1732 *Derby Mercury*. According to the article, a Mr Patrick Ryan broke into the house of a Quaker and set him on a gridiron over the fire until he was cooked alive. And an interesting story appears in the *Oxford Journal* from 1753, recalling how a Jewish patron of a public house in Leadenhall Street, London, brought with him his own gridiron to cook his meal on the fire. When he left to buy his victuals from the bar, his gridiron was used by another customer to cook pork steaks on (not very kosher). A huge row ensued in the pub and spilled out into the street, sadly not in favour of the Jewish patron who was told to take his custom elsewhere. This little news piece not only indicates that it was probably common for individuals to take their own utensils with them to cook food in public – out of necessity or personal choice – but that migrant communities such as the Jews were marginalised and discriminated against.

Salamander

A salamander goes under the name of a grill, gratiner, and brulee iron – basically anything that describes something that browns or caramelises the tops of food.

Spits

This is how meat was roasted – first by direct exposure to the fire and continuous motion/turning to avoid it burning, then in a closed oven. Mrs Beeton recommended spits be cleaned with sand and water. There was a wide range of spits, including the cradle spit, shaped like an elongated basket, and the infamous turnspit with its large hamster-like wheel mounted on the wall and powered by a small dog. Below is Mrs. Beeton's description of the bottle jack:

> The Bottle jack of which we here give an illustration with the wheel and hook and showing the precise manner of using it, is now commonly used in many kitchens. This consists of a spring enclosed in a brass cylinder and requires winding up before it is used and sometimes also during the operation of roasting. The joint is fixed to an iron hook which is suspended by a chain connected with a wheel and which in its turn is connected with the bottle jack. Beneath it stands the dripping pan which we have also engraved together with the basting ladle the use of which latter should not be spared as there can be no good roast without good basting. Spare the rod and spoil the child might easily be paraphrased into Spare the basting and spoil the meat. If the joint is small and light and so turns unsteadily this may be remedied by fixing to the wheel one of the kitchen weights. Sometimes this jack is fixed inside a screen but there is this objection to this apparatus that the meat cooked in it resembles the flavour of baked meat. This is derived from its being so completely surrounded with the tin that no sufficient current of air gets to it. It will be found preferable to make use of a common meat screen such as is shown in the woodcut. This contains shelves for warming plates and dishes and with this the reflection not being so powerful and more air being admitted to the joint the roast may be very excellently cooked.[3]

Above left: Victorian roasting jack.
Above right: Twentieth-century salamander.
Left: Twentieth-century Dutch oven. (Emma Kay)

Dutch ovens

Dutch ovens had two distinct types. The first is a simple cooking pot with a lid, buried in the hot coals of the fire. *Lloyds Encyclopædic Dictionary* reveals that this type of Dutch oven was still being used in America right up until the end of the nineteenth century, 'unsurpassed in its results with skilful housewives'. The other Dutch oven, or hastener, stood in front of the fire. Sometimes it had shelves or a hook to suspend meat from. There is an early advertisement by Stone & Co, as part of their complete kitchen set. Bought separately, the hastener cost around fourteen shillings and six pence in 1788, which would be in the region of £50 today.[4]

Miscellaneous Cookware

There is a vast range of small experimental appliances that were used to cook, from the late eighteenth to early twentieth centuries, from steaming to air drying and chemical cooking, portable cookers and experimental cookers. This is a genre worthy of a book in itself. Interestingly, a number of products that we are familiar with today were in use centuries before, like the *fromagère*, an early fondue, popular on the British dining table. A receptacle containing boiling water was balanced over an iron heater and then a covered dish containing cheese slices was placed on top. After around five minutes the

1950s cream and blue enamel saucepan and 1930s Oxo cube tin.

General Electric
toaster, 1950.
(Emma Kay)

cheese had melted and was served with anything from bread to vegetables and meat.[5]. Perforated ladles acted as early egg poachers, and before toasters, long forks were used to brown bread, crumpets and other baked products directly using the heat from the fire.

By the early 1900s, electric toasters were being produced for the domestic market. First engineered for mass consumption by the American firm General Electric, it was in fact the British who pioneered the invention of the electric toaster, initially advertised by the Essex based company, Crompton &Co., as early as 1893.[6] The first pressure cookers, a kitchen item I tend to associate the most with the 1940s, was also being used in kitchens during the early 1900s, as this article from the *Ballymena Observer* of 1923 instructs for cooking potatoes: 'A steam-pressure cooker is used, the simplest form consisting of a cylindrical iron tank with cone-shaped bottom to ensure drainage. Fifteen to twenty minutes' cooking under fifteen pounds' pressure is generally sufficient.'[7]

One of the most ingenious inventions in cooking, before temperatures could be regulated precisely when cooking times remained largely an exercise in guesswork, was the indicating cooking skewer of 1893. This handy device consisted of an ordinary skewer, surrounded by mercury and then given a brass frontage, with a basic indicator. The brass gauge marked the point at which the mercury should touch as soon as the meat reached its optimum temperature. It took around forty-five seconds from inserting the skewer into the meat to read the temperature from the rising mercury.[8] Never again would King Alfred be unfortunate enough to burn his cakes.

This chapter would not be complete without recognising, my own personal least-favourite item of modern twentieth century cooking inventions – the

This 2005 photograph of James Lovelock was taken by Bruno Comby of the Association of Environmentalists For Nuclear Energy.

microwave oven. Although the invention is frequently credited to the American physicist Percy Spencer, who developed the concept after the Second World War and was producing basic prototypes by the 1950s, it is James Lovelock, the British independent scientist who may indeed have been the first to successfully formulate microwave cooking. During a radio interview in 1954, as part of the iconic *Desert Island Discs* programme, then presented by Sue Lawley, Mr Lovelock revealed that many years earlier he had connected the output of a magnetron to a metal chamber containing a potato. There was a timer attached, which was set for ten minutes. It worked along the same principle as a microwave oven and cooked the potato, which he enjoyed for his lunch. Although Lovelock suggests he should take the credit, he is also humble about it and emphasises that there may have been many radar technicians who had undertaken the same experiment, but had never publicised it.[9]

6

Baking

I LOVE my Kitchen Aid mixer and hand blender, not just because they are heavy
duty and can make baking a little easier, but because they are design classics and look
amazing anywhere in a home or professional kitchen.

Paul A. Young, chocolatier,
Sick Children Trust, 2015

Of course before Mr Young began his baking career – and then some – there were
no Kitchen Aids or hand blenders – just good old-fashioned elbow grease. From the
1700s onwards, numerous bits of baking paraphernalia were being developed and
manufactured as a consequence of innovation and demand from certain strata of society
to improve and streamline their kitchens. William Adams & Son were considered the
principal mould makers and manufacturers of fine kitchen implements. With at least two
premises in London and connections in France, they were patronised by the best cooks.

Above: Iced cake *c.* 1920s.
Left: Pie making in 1914.

There was an auction advertised in Essex in 1839, targeting bakers and pastry cooks. The contents of a bake house were for sale including a ten-bushel oven, which would probably have been about eleven or twelve feet high, and eight feet wide. The weight of a bushel of coal varied depending on the region, with one London bushel equivalent to about eighty-three pounds of coal and a Cornish bushel around ninety-four pounds of coal. So a ten-bushel oven, such as the one advertised, would have had the capacity for anywhere between eight- and nine hundred pounds of coal to fuel it. Included in the sale were kneading troughs, roll and cake tins, biscuit cutters, jelly moulds, a muffin plate and 'dockers'. Originally an American invention, dockers were used to punch holes into biscuit dough prior to baking; they may have been used as a separate utensil, or feature as part of a biscuit mould or cutter itself. The objective of a docker was to ensure the biscuit mix did not rise and spoil – similar to our process of pricking pastry all over with a fork while baking blind. Dockers are still in use today, often as a roller or wheel covered in little spikes to make indentations in dough.[1]

The Home Yeast Company, Leeds, circulated advertisements after the First World War to recruit discharged soldiers to be retrained as tinsmiths to work in their baking utensil factory in Leeds. In addition to the Leeds company, there were several Home

Below left: Brioche cake tin from the early 1900s.
Top right: Late nineteenth-century tin biscuit cutter.
Bottom right: Nineteenth-century rice cake or biscuit mould. (Emma Kay)

Yeast Companies trading in Bedford, Northampton and Lincoln, amongst other locations during the 1920–30s, selling freezers and ice-cream powders. Whether it was the same company or not, I'm not sure, although the Northampton-based branch in 1915 boasted bread and cake tins, bun tins, and moulds crafted with 'real British workmanship'.[2]

It is safe to say that the level of manufacturing during this period was so prolific that there were literally hundreds and hundreds of competitors nationwide. Despite the many names that we are all familiar with today, these companies are, in the main, now all owned by one or two large multi-national corporations. The once thriving independent manufacturers of the centuries before are no longer a part of Britain's industrial baking society.

Bread and Cake Baking

Whilst early civilisations learnt to cook with fires by creatively mixing pulped grains of one type or another with water and cooking the mixture on hot stones to produce crude unleavened breads, the art of bread making in Britain was introduced by the Romans, who brought with them the first examples of risen products. Bakers remain one of the country's oldest culinary professions, with a Guild of Bakers established in London as early as 1155. Throughout history, the nation has had both a political and nutritional approach to bread's production and distribution. During the spectacularly adverse consequences of eighteenth century crop failures, the Prime Minister William Pitt called for all bread consumption to be replaced with that of rice and potatoes, so as to ration wheat for the greater needs of the military[3]. Brown bread and the use of coarse flours, once considered inferior, became a popular alternative at this time, even amongst the nobility. George III received the nickname 'Brown George'[4] for insisting that the royal household stocked brown bread. Even after Britain began to import large quantities of super fine flour from America, the coarser flours remained popular amongst the wealthier classes. In the twenty-first century, Britain has retained its obsession with bread, and there is a demand for new tastes by experimenting with less conventional flours such as spelt, rye, buckwheat and of course a range of gluten-free alternatives such as rice flour, potato flour and oat flour, to name a few. The latter two were once the traditional staple ingredients of bread making in Scotland and Ireland.

As bakers began to comprehend that too much heat from below would simply burn the bread underneath, without cooking it through, and that coarser floured breads required hotter ovens and longer cooking times, they became more sophisticated in ways to bake bread. Prior to the tin, most loaves were baked in a 'boule', a rustic handcrafted ball shape on a shovel-like wooden tool called a peel, or placed in large earthenware crocks. So much has already been written about the adulteration of baked goods throughout the eighteenth and nineteenth centuries but suffice it to say that the one-time popularity for very white breads, combined with the bakers' attempts to cut their costs led to extreme contamination in baking. More can be found about this subject, and its hero Friedrich Accum, in both *Dining with the Georgians* and *Dining with the Victorians*.

During the 1600s metal or wooden hoops, sometimes iron pans, were used to make yeast cakes, while patty pans and baking sheets were used for small cakes and biscuits.

The phrase bread tin, or loaf tin, was not commonly in use until the mid-1800s, although Elizabeth David notes that Eliza Rundell's 1807 edition of *A New System of Domestic Cookery*, is one of the earliest references to be found.[5] There has long been an association with bread poverty and war; the 'stuff of life', the one food that is cheap to produce and can sustain the masses.

The phrase 'patty pan' comes from the French word *pâté*, meaning paste, plus pan. Early ones were made from tinned steel and came in a variety of shapes and sizes and were used to make tartlets and small cakes. One of the more collectible of the range of small cake tins is the brioche mould of the early 1900s. Once tin had become the popular metal of choice in manufacturing, the word pan began to disappear, to be replaced with tin. It was certainly a word in common use by the 1920s. According to a story that appeared in the *Dundee Evening Telegraph* of 1921, a little German girl was travelling by train alone in a compartment and having realised the train had gone past her stop, opened the carriage door and held out a large 'cake tin' she had been carrying to break her fall as the train pulled away at some twenty miles an hour. She survived, despite serious injuries and shock.

One of the most prolific makers of baking tins during the early twentieth century, including the basic flan, tart, sponge finger and sandwich varieties, was H.J. Green & Co. Ltd., based in Brighton and established around 1910; it traded until 1948. The sweet, soft, spongy substance we are all familiar with and best known as 'cake' was not born until the mid-1700s. The types of cakes that were popular in the eighteenth century are somewhat removed from the standard chocolate, coffee, vanilla sponge, fruit, toffee or carrot cakes of today. Susannah Carter's The *Frugal Housewife, or Complete Woman Cook* of 1796 lists the following under 'all sorts of cakes': A Spanish Cake, Portugal Cake, Genoa Cake, Shrewsbury cakes, Marlborough Cakes, Uxbridge Cakes, Queen cakes, Pound cakes, Saffron cakes, Orange cakes, and so on. What is particularly noticeable here, as in other recipe books of the time, is the number of cakes named after countries or towns – cakes once synonymous with a region, but now largely forgotten. There's one particular cake that does not seem to have transcended into the twenty-first century, but was hugely popular during the 1920s, '30s and '40s. The Tango Cake (no relation to the branded fizzy fruit drink), perhaps named after the Argentinian tango, which had arrived in London during the first decade of the twentieth century and was taking the grand hotels with their tea dances by storm. It was a fruit cake, but that is about all the information I could find. One manufacturer of the Tango Cake was Peark's, which boasted some 653 branches of their cake shops across the country, and advertised it as being: '…just like a very fine home-made cake, rich but light and with plenty of fruit inside'.[6]

If the twenty-first century named its cakes in the same way as Britain once did, one wonders what they would be called – Bluetooth Cake, Facebook Cake, Apple Cake, (not the green shiny kind) Kindle Cake, or maybe even Posh & Becks Cake, Downton Abbey Cake or even Tom Hiddleston Cake. The possibilities are endless.

Biscuit Baking

Bis coctus is the Latin phrase for twice baked. Biscuits evolved out of refining simple ingredients into shapes and baking them for the purposes of sustenance on long journeys.

Left: Illustration of an eighteenth-century hot gingerbread vendor and his customers.

British sailors, as early as Tudor times, survived on a diet of 'ship's biscuits' made from flour, salt and water. They were pre-baked on land and then eaten soaked in stews or water. They would often have been laced with weevils and no doubt would have broken a tooth or two unless rehydrated.

According to Dan Foley's delightful book *Toys Through the Ages*, gingerbread was so popular in England that there were whole fairs dedicated to it, just retailing gingerbread and toys. Two of the most significant annual fairs took place in Birmingham right up until the nineteenth century; the tradition having its roots as early as the thirteenth century. There would have been long rows of market stalls selling gingerbread in every form, interspersed with booths for toys. Whilst gingerbread men were affectionately called 'Jim Crows' in America, they were referred to as 'husbands' in England. English shopkeepers would also stamp gingerbread and other baked goods with the maker's name, as both a novelty for the children and a useful means of advertising.[7] One of the most famous of London gingerbread street sellers was called 'Tiddy Doll', more about whom can be found in my book *Dining with the Georgians*.

The art of cutting biscuit mixtures into interesting shapes and embellishing them has been prevalent in British society for centuries. The word biscuit, associated with the sweet sophisticated products we know today was not in common use in Britain until the nineteenth century. Prior to this they were referred to as small cakes, or after specific treats like macaroons or Savoys (a sort of biscuit/cake). Savoys are a bit like Jaffa cakes in terms of the whole 'is it a cake or is it a biscuit' debate. There are early Georgian recipes where they are listed as cakes and then, somewhere between the Georgian and Victorian periods, they morph into biscuits. Here is a recipe from 1834, provided by a former cook to George IV, where they are most definitely biscuits:

Savoy Biscuit

Fourteen fine eggs, one pound of sugar, the zest of an orange, and seven ounces of potato flour. Put the whites of the eggs, which break one by one, lest there be a bad one, in an earthen pan, and the yolks in another. Weigh a pound of fine sugar, on which you have rubbed the zest of an orange; let it be perfectly dry when used. Put half a pound of this in the yolks, and stir them up, so as to leave no lumps add the remainder, and work it well twenty minutes; whip the whites very firm; but to prevent their turning to snow, add a good pinch of calcined and pulverised alum. When sufficiently whipped, which you will know by the whites forming little risings where the whisk is taken out, take some of them on the whisk, and mix them with the yolks; work the whites still, or they will turn to snow: pour the yolks gently to the whites, which stir with the whisk pass the whole through the tammy, and over this seven ounces of potato flour which mix as you pass it. The mixture should run from the spoon, forming a thread smooth and thin. Thin a few spoonfuls of the paste, which pour into the bottom of the mould, that no air may remain, which would cause air bubbles on the biscuit when done; put the remainder of the paste in the mould, and place it on a baking sheet; on this you previously put ashes an inch thick: put the biscuit in the middle of a moderate oven, which keep close an hour. Observe the biscuit: if it takes colour too fast put a few sheets of paper over it: in an hour take it out, if nicely coloured and firm to the touch, pass a baking sheet over the mould, turn it upside down and take it off; put a double band of paper round the bottom of the biscuit and tie it on: put the biscuit at the mouth of the oven a few minutes. Should the biscuit be soft to the touch when taken out continue to bake it till firm.[8]

Early tin biscuit cutters are the most valuable, and commonly had little holes cut in the back to help air circulate and aid the release of the dough from the cutter itself. Examples of early popular shapes include leaves, flowers, birds, animals, high-hatted men and ladies in long dresses. From 1900 to around 1930, stamped aluminium cutters were popular, followed by plastic products, from the 1940s onwards, with the earliest ones often transparent or in red and green. These would often be sold in sets and come stored in little hinge-lidded tins.

It also became fashionable to ice biscuits and after over a century of forcing bags, inserted with some metal funnels with which to pipe out designs, the syringe was introduced in the twentieth century. This made the process of icing somewhat easier, with the added bonus of different screw-on nozzles. The most popular of these new brands of icing kits were Nutbrown and Tala.

One other essential tool for biscuit making was the docker, still used today – although most domestic cooks tend to just use a fork. The docker looked like an instrument of torture with sharp spikes attached to a wooden handle. The dough was pierced full of holes before being baked to prevent any trapped air from making the biscuit bubble or rise up.

Tala icing set, *c.*1950–60, and 1940s flour sifter. (Emma Kay)

The Industrial Revolution heralded the fashion for mass-produced, commercial biscuits. Some of the biggest names of the nineteenth century like James Peek and George Frean, Joseph Huntley and George Palmer, William and Robert Jacob, the Fox family, George Burton and Thomas Tunnock are still familiar names today. Although most have faced years of takeovers and mergers, their names have remained legendary in biscuit manufacturing history, as have their inventions; the Garibaldi, the custard cream, the Bourbon cream, the cream cracker and the digestive, to name a few.

Pie Making

Pie making has its origins, like so many things, in Egyptian and Greek culinary history when grain mixtures would be moulded around honey and baked over coals, or meat was wrapped up in flour and water pastes to seal in the juices and flavours. In England the pie has thrived since at least the fourteenth century as a pastry dish, originally filled with magpies. Hence the name.

Elizabeth Raffald's charmingly titled *Observations on Pies* in her 1806 edition of *The Experienced English Housekeeper*, informs us that:

> Raised pies should have a quick oven, and well closed up, or your pie will fall in the sides; it should have no water put in till the minute it goes to the oven, it makes the crust sad, and is a great hazard of the pie running. Light paste requires a moderate oven, but not too slow, it will make it sad; and a quick oven will catch and burn it,

and not give it time to rise; tarts that are iced require a slow oven, or the icing will be brown and the paste not be baked. These sort of tarts ought to be made of sugar-paste, and rolled very thin.[9]

Early pies were moulded into shapes using wooden hoops. By the Victorian period any dish deep enough to contain a filling and be topped with a crust lid was used to make pies – dishes made from tin and earthenware. You could also buy pie dish 'collars', either in white or of various colours, designed to be secured around the pie for decorative purposes. The company Coles & Owen were one of the top manufactures of these collars. The Victorian era also popularised the pie funnel. These little, often decorative, items were placed in the centre of the pie to support the crust itself, release steam and prevent the pie juices from boiling over. The quintessential bird-shaped funnels that we are all familiar with did not emerge until the 1930s. Sadly, pie funnels now appear to have become nothing more than collector's items as people tended to stop using them regularly around the 1950s.

Miscellaneous Baking Tools

The rolling pin and pastry jigger or cutter represent two of the earliest sophisticated baking tools, with a provenance of at least the 1600s and probably earlier. Glass rolling pins, like those produced at the famous Nailsea glass factory near Bristol, were symbols of good fortune and would be kept on board ships by superstitious sailors, alongside their hand-made pastry jiggers carved from scrimshaw on long, lonely, sea journeys as gifts for wives or sweethearts.[10] Rolling pin shapes and sizes have varied considerably over the centuries, with glass ones often filled with ice to maintain a cold pastry, grooved or scored ones designed to crush oats and the French rolling pins of the Victorian era that were thicker in the middle then tapered at the ends, making the process of rotating and rolling dough easier. The smallest rolling pins were used for confectionery or fine, delicate, pastry work. In 1866 two Americans – Theodore Williamson and Chas Richardson – applied for a patent for their unique rolling pin, designed to combine a number of different uses, namely as a rolling pin, grater, steak tenderiser and butter print. The rolling pin consisted of sections with special adapters to carry out the multitude of tasks.[11] It's unlikely that this particular utensil ever took off in the commercial market as I have not come across anything similar. However, in today's competitive and labour-saving gadget society, it actually seems like quite a good concept, were it not for the fact that we no longer really use butter prints, but an alternative icing stencil or pattern cutter might well prove successful in this interesting cooking combo.

The iconic Tala icing sets, synonymous with the 1950s, were actually being manufactured and sold as early as 1931. Whilst the packaging changed from a tin box to a cardboard one; the principle remained the same, with a set comprising an icing syringe and six assorted nozzles. Some later versions also included a metal turntable to assist with icing cakes. The metal syringe was a huge breakaway from the piping bags of the centuries before. At two shillings and sixpence in 1931, equivalent to about £6 today, they were also a reasonably affordable kitchen luxury.

Flour and sugar dredgers or sifters were also tools regularly used in the baking process, as early as the late Georgian period, originally cast in silver, then tin and then made in ceramics. A silver dredger was one of the items recorded in a staged robbery and subsequent murder of the MP Lord William Russell in 1840, by his Swiss valet, interestingly called Courvoisier.[12] It is understood that the writers Charles Dickens and William Makepeace Thackeray were present at Courvoisier's public execution; both were against capital punishment. Dickens wrote of the execution:

> I did not see one token in all the immense crowd ... of any one emotion suitable to the occasion ... No sorrow, no salutary terror, no abhorrence, no seriousness; nothing but ribaldry, debauchery, drunkenness, and flaunting vice in fifty other shapes ... It was so loathsome, pitiful and vile a sight, that the law appeared to be as bad as he, or worse.[13]

Nineteenth-century Nailsea painted glass rolling pin and wooden pastry jigger. (Emma Kay)

7

Moulds

There are a few tricks that will help you make sophisticated jellies and avoid disaster.
For unmoulded jellies forget what it says on the back of the pack of gelatine and use
one leaf of gelatine per 100ml of jelly. Avoid pretty antique ceramic moulds – you'll
have a tough time getting the jelly out, though there is a trick for this.

Sam Bompas and Harry Parr, Jellymongers
The Guardian, 'Jelly Clinic: how to deliver a quiver', 15 June 2010

From early Chinese rice cakes to complicated French decorative haute cuisine, moulds
have been integral to any kitchen collection to sculpt ice, confectionary, jellies and aspics,
small cakes and biscuits – basically anything that can be shaped into a pleasing form for
display or merely pleasure. One of the most curious of English cake moulds is that of the
Biddenden Chulkhurst twins. Legend has it that in a little wooded village sometime in the
twelfth century, twin girls were born joined at the hip and shoulders. Having bequeathed
local land for the benefit of the poor on their death, it became a tradition each Easter to
dole out cakes (more like hard biscuits) shaped in the image of the twins. This story has
been researched, and dismissed as folklore; researched some more, re-dated to around
the 1500s; then dismissed again. The town has thrived off the charitable lands and it
became a local tourist attraction during the Victorian era. Whether the story is myth or
not the practice of distributing Biddenden twin-shaped cakes has survived in the village,
whose inhabitants remain proud of its tradition. If you ever come across an old mould
of conjoined twin girls whilst routing around the charity shops of Kent, you'll know you
have potentially struck gold.

Hornbooks

Alongside traditional gingerbread moulds, hornbooks are perhaps some of the oldest
in this category. Hornbooks were an educational tool for children that spanned the
sixteenth and nineteenth centuries. They consisted of a single sheet of alphabet letters,
mounted on wood or leather, protected by a surface of horn and with a handle for easy
carrying. Often they also contained Roman numerals. It became customary to make

edible hornbooks not long after they became popular. The seventeenth-century poet Matthew Prior wrote about this in his *Poems On Several Occasions*, noting:

To Master John the English Maid
A Horn-book gives of Ginger-bread:
And that the child may learn the better,
As He can name, He eats the Letter.

Above:
Gingerbread
hornbook moulds.
Left:
Nineteenth-century
ice-cream mould
and earthenware
jelly mould.

Gingerbread hornbooks and battledore books (similar to the hornbook, but with the letters of the alphabet jumbled up, to aid learning and including a small prayer or story) were particularly popular in the eighteenth century, with London street sellers offering them at around half a penny a slice.[1]

Right: Twentieth-century wax Springerle mould.
Below: Twentieth-century wooden Springerle mould.

Springerles

Essentially a Springerle is a German biscuit or small cake mould that comes in all shapes and sizes, most typically as a board with simple symbolic motifs or intricately carved designs. It is also one of the oldest of moulds, most popular from the sixteenth century onwards, but in existence well before then. They were originally made of wood and wax, and sometimes sculpted into a rolling pin to provide a continuous imprint onto dough. The traditional dough for Springerle moulds does alter slightly from recipe to recipe, but most are flavoured with anise. The Springerle either acquired its name from the springy consistency of the biscuit mould, or literally translates as 'little jumper' or 'little knight', perhaps with reference to early designs.

These moulds became popular throughout Europe. A traditional recipe can be found in *German National Cookery for English Kitchens*, 1873:

> Half a pound of fine flour, half a pound of sifted sugar, two eggs, an ounce of butter, and a pinch of carbonate of soda dissolved in a teaspoonful of milk, or a little more if necessary.
>
> Form with these a dough, which must be well kneaded. Roll it out a quarter of an inch thick.
>
> Mix the anise-seeds into the dough... The more general way of moulding the springerle is with various figures cut in wooden blocks. These are dusted with flour, the paste rolled out and cut into small pieces, which are then pressed into the shapes, the surface shaved off with a knife, and the devices turned out by knocking the blocks as they are held upside down. Bake them very pale.[2]

Jelly and Blancmange

From as early as the Egyptians, people have been cooking with gelatine. Once the delight of only the wealthy, it is thought to have been a Frenchman, sometime during the seventeenth century, who first widely communicated the process of boiling animal bones to acquire gelatine. However, the first adhesive extracted from fish bones was patented in 1750 by the British.[3]

Blancmange is considered an invention of the Middle East, a sort of gelatinous concoction involving almond milk, chicken, rice and sugar, and introduced to Europe, like many other culinary revolutions, by the Crusaders.[4] By the fourteenth and fifteenth century, cream and eggs were added to create an appetising first course. This was the first use of the term blanc-manger, or white food. By the end of the Medieval period, the meat was removed and by the nineteenth century, a number of trial and error recipes based on this foundation dish using gelatine, cornflour and arrowroot eventually produced the type of blancmange that we are all familiar with today.[5] This 600 year or so culinary evolution makes blancmange quite a special dish.

Many recipe books of the nineteenth century cite isinglass as the predominant gelatine agent in cooking and baking. This was an early form of widely-used gelatine obtained from the bladder of fishes. By the mid- to late 1800s the term 'gelatine' starts to appear, signifying a transcendence from fish to meat bones, most likely calves' feet gelatine, which was the cheapest on the market. Until well into the second half of the nineteenth century moulds for deserts and decorative table dishes were only used by the very wealthy. As mentioned in my book *Dining with the Georgians*, it wasn't until the 1851 Crystal Palace Great Exhibition was staged, showcasing a wealth of jelly moulds in a variety of shapes, that the mould became generally popular across a variety of households.

Moulds were often formed from copper, tin, pewter or glass; but silver was the most common early form of mould during the 1600s; the earthenware mould was not developed until the latter part of the eighteenth century by the pioneering pottery company Wedgewood.

Animals were once the most popular design for jellies, possibly because they were generally created for the pleasure of children. In fact, until the mid-nineteenth century, moulds were simply referred to as 'shapes'. In her *Complete Confectioner* of 1783, Hannah Glasse acknowledges this by writing: 'Pour jelly into what thing pleases to shape it and when cold, turn it out'.

Moulds were the playthings of nobility. The fashionable classes made individual entrees into tiny delicate images of cutlets, tongues and small chickens. There were also treats like flavoured ices and sweetmeats, made into elaborate displays as centrepieces on mirrored glass or to adorn fanciful cakes and puddings. A century later and every aspiring middle-class household had a kitchen complete with a set of perhaps as many as one hundred moulds, all cast in different materials for different purposes.

John Massey a confectioner who had premises in Cambridge Street, London, with his son William, wrote two successful books focussing on puddings and ices. Their business was to dress tables for suppers, balls and wedding breakfasts. Their particular specialty was incorporating 'The Alexandra Bouquet' into their table settings. This was, amongst other things, an arrangement of peonies, hydrangeas and roses. Their biscuit, ice, and compote book provides a suggested list of ice moulds for the kitchen, which includes the following, and hopefully provides an indication of the scale of utensils available in just this one niche category:

Apricot, Peach or Apple Ice Mould
Bomb Ice Mould
Cedratti Ice Moulds – a citrus Italian fruit
Frozen Stand Mould – a circular tin mould
Grape Ice Mould
Ice Moulds for Dessert – long, pewter and ornamental

Melon Ice Mould
Massey's Bomb Ice Mould (with the addition of a comedy fuse on top)
Orange Ice Mould
Plum Ice Moulds
Pear Ice Moulds
Pine Apple Ice Mould
Rusk Mould (in the shape of a common brick)[6]

A much smaller list of generic moulds, essential for the kitchen appears in the writings of one of the most well-known 'celebrity chefs' of the Victorian age, Alexis Soyer – his iconic *Gastronomic Regenerator* was first published in 1846:

Baba and sponge cake moulds
Pie moulds
Jelly and charlotte moulds

Small jelly and dariole mould (perhaps a dariole flowerpot-shaped mould).

Pie Moulds

The pie is one dish that Britain can really call its own. For centuries it has delighted consumers with its rich, raised, decorative borders on the lids of its shallow pie dish offerings of meat, fish or fruit. From rooks, to rats and gooseberries, the British have experimented with many fillings throughout history, all topped with a crust. Centuries ago pies were often symbolic and bold, with images of flowers, beasts and heraldic family crests. They were marked and stamped – given an identity by bakers cooking for the public, many of whom until the late nineteenth or early twentieth century were without their own oven. Unlike other decorative moulds, the large, stately, embellished pie moulds of the eighteenth and nineteenth centuries, when pastry making was more of an artistic medium, have become obsolete. Despite this, there has been a recent revival of traditional pie-making, with the iconic shapes and flourished crusts reappearing in the supermarkets and farmers' markets. The fiery Anglo-Italian celebrated cook of the Victorian and late Georgian age, and one-time head chef to Queen Victoria, Charles Elmé Francatelli, published a recipe for Capon Pie with Truffles, in his successful *Modern Cook* of 1845. This is a traditional and extravagant pie without the need of a mould – hence the original use of the word 'raised' which means the wall and structure were built up by hand, before pie moulds existed, a bit like creating something on a potter's wheel.

Capon Pie with Truffles

'FIRST bone a capon, spread it out on the table and season the inside with prepared spices and a little salt, then spread a layer of force meat of fat livers and place upon this in alternate rows some square fillets or strips of fat, bacon tongue and truffles, cover these with a layer of the force meat, repeat the strips of bacon then fold both sides of the skin over each other so as to give to the capon a plump appearance and set it aside on a dish.

The difference between a raised pie and a timbale consists principally in the former being raised by hand or otherwise with a stiff paste while the latter is prepared in a mould lined with a more delicate kind of short crust, which is made edible.

Next pare off the sinewy skin from the mouse piece or inner part of a leg of veal, daube it with seasoned lardoons of fat bacon then place this and an equal quantity of dressed ham with the capon.

Prepare four pounds of hot water paste. Take two thirds of this mould it into a round ball on the slab with the palm of the hand and then roll it out in the form of a band about two feet long and six inches wide, trim the edges and pare the ends square, taking care to cut them in a slanting direction, wet them with a paste brush dipped in water mixed with a little flour and wrap them over one another neatly and firmly so as to show the join as little as possible.

Next roll out half the remainder of the paste either in a circular or oval form about a quarter of an inch thick to the size the pie is intended to be made, place this with buttered paper under it on a baking sheet, wet it round the edge with a paste brush dipped in water and stick a narrow band of the paste about half an inch high all round it, to within about an inch of the edge the wall or crust of the pie is to be raised up round this, and by pressing on it with the tips of the fingers it should be made to adhere effectually to the foundation. Then by pressing the upper part of the pie with the foundation. Then by pressing the upper part of the pie with the fingers and thumbs of both hands it will acquire a more elegant appearance somewhat resembling the curved lip of a vase. The base must be spread out in proportion to the top by pressing on it with the thumb.

The bottom and sides of the pie should now be lined with a coating of force meat of fat livers. Or if preferred with veal and fat bacon in equal proportions, well-seasoned, chopped fine and pounded, next place in the veal and ham previously cut up in thick slices and well-seasoned and fill up the cavity with some of the force meat, then add the capon and cover it over and round with the remainder of the force meat, placing some truffles in with it and cover the whole with thin layers of fat bacon.

Roll out the remainder of the paste and after wetting this and the round the edges, use it to cover in the pie, pressing the edges of both tightly with the fingers and thumb in order to make them adhere closely together, trim the edge neatly and pinch it round with the pastry pincers.

The pie should then be egged over and decorated for which latter purpose a similar kind of paste must be used, being first rolled out thin then cut out in the form of leaves, half-moons, rings &c and arranged according to the designs contained in [No 249] or if preferred according to the designs contained in [No 249], or if preferred a moulding raised from decorating boards with some of the paste may be used instead.

The pie must then be placed in the oven and baked for about four hours, and when done should be withdrawn and about a pint of strongly reduced consommé made from the carcasses of the capons, two calves feet and the usual seasoning should be introduced within it through a funnel, it must then be kept in a cold place until wanted for use, when the cover should be carefully removed without breaking it, and after the top of the pie has been decorated with some bright aspic jelly it may be put on again and sent to table.

Note: For making pies of turkeys fowls pheasants grouse partridges &c follow the above directions.[7]

Confectionery

One of the main categories of the culinary trade concerning the use of moulds is confectionery. There were many highly-skilled Continental craftsmen who brought their talents to Britain during the eighteenth century, setting up establishments such as confectioners and pastry shops. New substances from overseas like agar (Japan) and arrowroot (West Indies) enabled us to experiment with confectionery and jelly. Traditional almond sweetmeats were transformed into a variety of moulded starchy mixtures incorporating milk, sugar and flavourings to make blancmanges, bon-bons, sugar plums, candied fruits and so on. Delicate shapes and fancies were moulded from gum paste prepared from tragacanth (trag a gan ath), a natural gum taken from the sap of a plant from the Middle East. It is also what is commonly used in the sugar pastes that we continue to use today in sugar crafting. Tragacanth would have come in large, hard chunks that look a bit like dark-red crystallised ginger and would then be ground down in a mortar.

There were nearly 7,000 trading pastry cooks and confectioners listed in the 1841 census for Great Britain. Although this figure sits just in the Victorian era, it's clear these businesses were established well before then, with confectioners trading in the city of Leeds alone as early as 1817. But you'd be hard pushed to find one or two there on the high street today.

One of the biggest names in confectionery during the Georgian era was James Gunter, who went into partnership with an Italian confectioner, Domenico Negri, in a shop in Berkeley Square called the Pot and Pineapple. It later became a fashionable early teashop

Left: Jarrin cooking tools.

in the 1830s, run by James's son, one of the few establishments where ladies could go and drink tea unchaperoned. By 1843, it was trading as Gunter & Co.

William Jarrin worked as an ornamental confectioner for James Gunter, but also had his own confectioners in New Bond Street. He wrote the lovely and descriptive The *Italian Confectioner* around 1822, which includes some of his tools of the trade. Amongst others these included a tin syringe or 'rammer' with which you secured different shaped templates on to the bottom to force out shapes like stars or flowers. This would perhaps have been used to make little almond paste biscuits. A selection of small modelling shaped moulds was essential and, once crafted in gum, these moulded shapes would hang on a makeshift line to dry. Iron wafer makers were also part of Jarrin's confectioner's tool kit. This piece of equipment was placed on the fire to heat, rubbed with butter or pork rind, then the batter would be poured into it, taking care to cover the engraved part, closed, placed on the fire and turned until it was evenly cooked. You would then remove the wafer and immediately shape it around a piece of rounded wood. There were also tin funnels used to pipe out small biscuits, and boxwood moulds to create shapes that resembled small baskets.

Jarrin's store obviously wasn't as successful as Gunter's as he was declared insolvent just a year after writing his book, and at the same time as filing for a patent for a new apparatus that he invented to cool liquids. He died at the age of sixty-four, in 1848.

The types of cakes, pastries and confections that were produced for the wealthy and burgeoning middle classes during the Georgian age were very elaborate, technically and visually pleasing. Even butter pats were stamped or had decorative borders, biscuits and sweets were moulded into intricately carved designs.

Victorian chocolate egg mould.

8

Utensils

The Bake-Off-winner-turned-food-writer can't live without his offset (or angled) spatula.
'I have about seven of them. It's like an extension of my hand. For recipes such as
my salted caramel brownie, which has a layer of salted caramel through the middle,
you have to make sure that you have a nice level layer of brownie mix, and it's great
for that. People ask me how to get a flat, professional finish on a cake, and an offset
spatula, together with a cake turntable, are the secrets.'

Ed Kimber, former Bake-Off winner

Daily Telegraph, 19 March 2016

The word 'spatula' is one we tend to associate with the plastic revolution of the 1950s
but this word has been a feature of the English language since the sixteenth century.
These utensils are often called cake turners, or a slice, in the United States. Spatulas were
originally designed in wood or metal. They were used to scrape, stir, transfer and apply
different solutions, chemicals and potions. Kitchen specific spatulas are cited in recipe
books from the early 1800s. Before this, its cousin, the wooden spoon, was usually on
hand to stir, mix and move ingredients. When pickling gherkins, Georgian culinary
legend Hannah Glasse instructs that once stored in a bladder and a leather, the pickles
themselves should only ever be removed with a wooden spoon.[1]

Working in a 1920s household, the author Margaret Powell wrote extensively in
her many published memoires about the ups and downs of domestic service on her
journey from lowly kitchen maid to cook. When she first started her job, Margaret was
surprised and confessed ignorance about the number of cooking utensils needed to run
a large-scale kitchen:

> There were knives of all kinds, all shapes and sizes, big long carving knives, small
> knives for paring fruit, pallet knives, bent knives for scraping out basins with, and then
> metal spoons, not the ordinary type – they were like a kind of aluminium – coloured
> spoon – huge ones, about six of them. The largest ones had the measures on them, from
> ounces right up to dessert-spoonfuls ... two sieves, a hair sieve and a wire sieve, and a
> flour sifter, and an egg whisk ... Then there were two kinds of graters, one fine one for
> nutmegs, and one to do the breadcrumbs on; there was a big chopping board and a
> small chopping board, three or four kinds of basins ...[2]

Fig. 115.—Kitchen and Table Utensils: —1, Carving-knife (Sixteenth Century); 2, Chalice or Cup, with Cover (Fourteenth Century); 3, Doubled-handled Pot, in Copper (Ninth Century); 4, Metal Boiler, or Tin Pot, taken from "L'Histoire de la Belle Hélaine" (Fifteenth Century); 5, Knife (Sixteenth Century); 6, Pot, with Handles (Fourteenth Century); 7, Copper Boiler, taken from "L'Histoire de la Belle Hélaine" (Fifteenth Century); 8, Ewer, with Handle, in Oriental Fashion (Ninth Century); 9, Pitcher, sculptured, from among the Decorations of the Church of St. Benedict, Paris (Fifteenth Century); 10, Two-branched Candlestick (Sixteenth Century); 11, Cauldron (Fifteenth Century).

Above left: Sixteenth-century utensils.
Above right: Kitchen utensils, 1939.
Below: Vintage cutlery.

Margaret was even more surprised to learn from the under-housemaid Mary, when seeing them all laid out to make lunch, that 'you've not seen anything'. And she was right, this list doesn't even scratch the surface of the level of equipment that was required in the kitchens of the wealthy.

Some fifty years before, Mrs Beeton wrote the following about utensils of the past–bearing in mind that the word utensils then, covered most everyday cooking equipment:

> Of the culinary utensils of the ancients, our knowledge is very limited; but as the art of living, in every civilized country, is pretty much the same, the instruments for cooking must, in a great degree, bear a striking resemblance to each other. On referring to classical antiquities, we find mentioned among household utensils, leather bags, baskets constructed of twigs, reeds and rushes; boxes, basins and bellows; bread moulds, brooms and brushes; cauldrons, colanders, cisterns and chafing-dishes; cheese-rasps, knives and ovens of the Dutch kind; funnels and frying-pans; hand-mills, soup ladles, milk pails and oil jars, presses, scales and sieves, spits of different sizes…spoons, fire-tongs, trays, trenchers and drinking-vessels…This enumeration, if it does nothing else, will, to some extent, indicate the state of the simpler kinds of mechanical arts among the ancients.[3]

Small items of kitchenware have been highly prized throughout history. The Kings Room at Oxburgh Hall in Norfolk features a stunning stained glass window illustrating a domestic scene of a couple surrounded by an array of kitchen utensils from the sixteenth and seventeenth century. There have been numerous works of art over the years that have captured the quirkiness of kitchen utensils, like the print titled *Implements animated in the kitchen* in the collections at the Science Museum and Thomas Tegg's 1811 print *Dedicated to the Housemaids and Cooks of the United Kingdom*. Tegg's picture depicts two people entirely composed of small kitchen implements. Probably the most famous are the paintings of the seventeenth century artist Cornelis Delff whose series of kitchen still life paintings visually capture both the variety, colours and quality of early utensils.

Skyline, Nutbrown, Tala and Prestige represent some of the best-known smaller kitchen utensil and gadget manufacturers of the early twentieth century. One of the oldest of these is Tala, a late Victorian company originally called Taylor Law & Co. Ltd. (Can you see now how the name Tala arose?) Nutbrown was established in 1932 and Skyline in the 1940s. Tala and Nutbrown are enjoying something of a revival and even the classic elements of the Skyline range have recently been reproduced and sold by Lakeland.

Lemon Squeezers

In America they are called reamers and there are large serious groups of dedicated collectors across the United States. Collecting what the British call hand-held juicers, or sometimes squeezers, is less popular, but the shape, size and variety over time makes them a fascinating utensil in many respects. From wood, to glass, to ceramic and aluminium they have also been cast in just about every type of material. Early wooden squeezers were commonly used in kitchens from the 1820s–30s, described here in detail from French Domestic Cookery: 'The Lemon-Squeezer is made of wood; by inserting it in half a lemon and moving it round, the juice will immediately flow out. The head is deeply fluted…This implement is common in Belgium, as well as in England.'[4]

1940s ceramic lemon squeezer. (Emma Kay)

Ice-Cream Scoop

It would be a twenty-nine-year-old African American who would pioneer the first patent in 1897 for that most fabulous of kitchen gadgets – the ice-cream scoop. Alfred Cralle was a porter at both a hotel and a pharmacy before inventing his 'ice-cream mould and disher'.[5] It was his job that inspired Cralle to design the scoop, as he found it difficult to dig frozen ice-cream out of containers.

Mashers, Ricers and Sieves

The phrase 'potato masher' didn't become popular until the late Georgian period of the 1820s. Early versions were wooden and looked a bit like a giant toadstool or a large pestle, literally designed to pummel vegetables or fruit into a pulp. By the 1930s, a more sophisticated metal zigzag implement attached to a wooden handle, like the instantly recognisable Skyline or Nutbrown products, became the more popular design and one that most of us are familiar with in our own kitchens today.

Potato ricers didn't come into use in Britain until around 1900. It is similar to a garlic press except larger; the potato is forced out of perforated holes, providing a smooth finish. Some ricers are conical shaped and a wooden pestle was used to force the potato through the holes. These type of sieves were more general and could have been used for anything from forcing a variety of vegetables, gravies and stocks, to jam-making. The iconic mid-twentieth century Wearever conical sieve that rested on a tripod of legs was an American concept, which made its way into some British kitchens.

One of the earliest forms of British sieve, was the Tamis or Tammy, a device that originally looked like skipping rope handles attached either side to a piece of mesh cloth. This kitchen tool required a person to hold either end and to turn and twist it so liquids and pulps were pushed through the cloth. Later, a Tammy evolved into more of a circular snare drum, made of wood or metal, supporting tightly strung horsehair and later nylon mesh. By the 1890s most middle-class kitchens would have possessed a number of colanders, with a variety of perforated patterns, cast in a variety of materials from copper to enamelled iron.

Larding Pins and Skewers

Larding pins and kitchen picks, were essential utensils in the kitchen and were undoubtedly adopted from the French by the English to skewer and flavour meat from the 1700s onwards. Larding pins were anywhere from six inches to a foot in length, pointed at one end while the other had a sort of tweezer mechanism with a cleft or an 'eye', similar to that of a needle. They were made of brass or steel. Bacon fat was cut into strips, depending on the size of the joint of meat, then fed through the eye of the pin before being inserted into the meat and drawn out the other end, leaving about an inch of fat sticking out either end. Poultry tended to be larded across the breast. From the nineteenth century, larding needles came in decorative tin or japanned cases, with a sharpening tool.[6] As Eliza Acton stated: 'Larding the surface of meat, poultry or game, gives it a good appearance, but it is a more positive improvement to meat of a dry nature to interlard the inside with large lardoons of well-seasoned delicate, striped English bacon'.[7]

Whisks

The typical balloon wire whisk of today was thought to have been the invention of the French some time in the mid-nineteenth century. It is understood that the first mechanical egg beater was patented by another African-American inventor, Willis Johnson, in 1884. In fact, it was much more than an egg beater. Willis' invention was an early machine for mixing eggs, batters and all sorts of other ingredients with two double-acting chambers, to enable the cook to mix several batches of ingredients simultaneously. A much earlier version of his beaters, which were more of a churn, were marketed, distributed and sold via a three-man partnership that became messy, complicated, and ended in a lawsuit overseen by none other than a young Abraham Lincoln. The case left Johnson with no share of the profits, with a product that was branded worthless in court – 'A dismal failure of a machine.'[8] However, perhaps this was the spark for the fire that would lead to Johnson's successful egg beater some forty years later.

Britain began to invent rotary-style, hand-held kitchen utensils around 1860 but nothing on the scale of Johnson's complex and intelligent machine. E.P. Griffiths was one of the first with his compound-action egg whisk and batter mixer, priced at 30 shillings in 1861.[9] At around £1,500 in today's currency, it certainly remained a luxury labour-saving device for the wealthy. Whilst America had cornered the market and even boasted a well-known brand of beaters, 'Dover' beaters, by the 1890s, Britain struggled to popularise this type of item for the masses but, by 1910, the market was flooded with patented egg beaters.

Once again it would be the Americans that would pioneer electric mixers as early as 1908; the engineering firm Hobart's were the originators of the first Kitchen Aid domestic mixer in 1919. It would be another thirty years before Mr Kenneth Wood, a British wartime electronics engineer who turned his hand to domestic appliances, would be able to rival the American and European market with his legendary Kenwood Chef.[10] An early advertisement for the Kenwood Chef bills it as 'simply amazing' in its abilities to mince, mix, beat, blend, whip and extract. And one would hope so, as it sold at the equally amazing price of nearly £29.00, which would be around £800 today.[11] Incidentally Kenneth's grandfather was the genius behind Maynard's Wine Gums and Kenneth himself was also the founder of Forest Mere Health Farm, now one of the four world-famous Champneys resorts in the UK.

Miscellaneous Utensils

There is a myriad of small, helpful devices in the kitchen that can be classified as utensils. Cooling racks, for instance, have always fascinated me as they are such an essential item for the kitchen but perhaps not the sexiest. In Alexis Soyer's 1847 *Gastronomic Regenerator* he talks about the need for a cooling shelf, which either suggests the phrase 'cooling rack' had not yet been invented or that simply a shelf in the coolest part of the kitchen was best for getting hot items down to the right temperature.[12] The first mention of the phrase 'cooling rack' in a domestic kitchen context that I have been able to find appears in 1894, in Alfred Stefferud's *Yearbook of Agriculture*.[13] Stefferud instructs that 'cakes, cookies, and pies placed on a cooling rack after removal from the oven cool quickly because air can circulate underneath as well as around.' This is also an American publication and America did have the tendency to lead in the area of kitchenalia innovation during the nineteenth century.

The *Dublin Express* of 1886 includes an article on bread making and describes how the hot bread is immediately placed on cooling racks. Similarly, the *Birmingham Daily Post* of 1890 lists a number of items for a confectioners, recently gone into liquidation. These include bon-bon and chocolate cooling racks, so clearly they were being used for industrial-scale confectionary in the latter part of the nineteenth century.[14] By the 1920–30s the cooling rack had become a popular item in the kitchen, often made of decorative fancy wire-work, moulded into lots of different shapes, unlike the rather dowdy standard rectangular ones of today.

The fish slice and the cake slice appear to have evolved together as trowel-shaped utensils of the 1700s, perhaps because fish was often served in puddings (see May recipe below). Although the modern-day fish slice has come to resemble more of a slotted spatula, the cake slicer/server has remained true to its original design. They were once both highly decorated with patterns and engravings inspired by the Middle East and the Orient, crafted in silver.

Fruit cakes became the symbol of fertility during the seventeenth and eighteenth centuries, with all of the symbolism attached to the cake itself; how the top tier of the wedding cake needed to be kept back to save for the couple's christening of their first child and the custom for the bride and groom to cut the cake – the first act they would complete together as man and wife. By the late 1600s, the bridal cake (more of a pastry sandwich) was developed from an old custom of baking a bride pye. One of the oldest recipes for a Bride Pye is recorded in Robert May's *The Accomplished*

Cook in 1671. It contains oysters, so maybe a fish/cake slice would have been used to serve it.

> Provide cocks-stones and combs, or lamb-stones and sweet-breads of veal, a little set in hot water and cut to pieces, also two or three ox-pallets blanched and sliced, a pint of oysters. Sliced dates, a handful of pine kernels, a little quantity of broom-buds pickled. Some fine inter-larded bacon sliced, nine or ten chestnuts roasted and blanched, season them with salt, nutmeg, and some large mace, and close it up with some butter, with three yolks of eggs, some white or claret wine, the juice of a lemon or two, cut up the lid, and pour on the lear, shaking it well together; then lay on the meat, sliced lemon and pickled barberries, and cover it again, let the ingredients be put into the middle or scollops of the pie.[15]

What is thought to be the world's oldest wedding cake dates back to the 1890s and originating from the CH Philpott family bakers in Basingstoke. It can be found on display in Basingstoke's Willis Museum. I would very much like to know what they cut it with.

A Second World War 'Bully Beef' tin opener. (Emma Kay)

9

Serving

Think ceramic plates with a beautiful flecked glaze finish, fine crystal wine glasses and
wooden table accessories that are perfect for sharing and saving space on your table.
Advertising for Jason Atherton's new range of tableware, Social

Cutlery

Cutlery is perhaps the most versatile and multi-purpose of all kitchenalia collectibles.
Georgian silver is amongst the most elaborate. During the reign of George I and George II,
it is characterised by its rococo designs of elegant silver swirls, curves and frills. By the
reign of George III, the classic and more simplistic Revival style was adopted.

Victorian cutlery was mostly machine-made and could therefore adapt to numerous
styles from Middle Eastern to Indian and Egyptian. The official catalogue of the 1851
Great Exhibition illustrates that electroplated, rather than solid silver, items for the table
were the most fashionable at this time.

Nature influenced table settings with the addition of flowers and floral displays, tea
pots with branch handles and fruit-shaped ceramics.[1] The Victorian era was a time of
great novelty in design and saw the beginning of the hugely romantic art nouveau style.

The demand for modern designs and materials continued, until it peaked in the
1950s. Mass-produced stainless steel cutlery as well as EPNS ware in slim and elegant
light-weight styles replaced the individual elegance of centuries past. Gone were the
bone handles and the heavy long-bladed knives with their time-consuming sharpeners.

Forks were not commonly used in England until around the middle of the 1500s,
although they were more common across Europe, with references dating as far back as the
eleventh century. Perhaps forks were popularised by the Italians with their pasta eating
ways. But not in Venice, apparently, where it is believed one of the first-ever references
to forks was made. According to local records a 'Byzantine lady' arrived in Venice as a
new bride sometime in the eleventh century. She brought with her a golden two-pronged
fork, which caused a great sensation because St Peter Damian, later known as the Bishop
of Ostia, mentioned it in one of his sermons, sternly rebuking the lady in public for her
extravagant, unholy ways, noting God had given her fingers for that very purpose. In fact,
the presence of the finger-bowl on some restaurant tables, undoubtedly harkens back to

a time when we all ate with our fingers and would use the basin and ewer to wash at the table between courses. It was spoons that first supplemented the use of fingers, which perhaps explains the old custom of godparents giving spoons as a gift at baptisms.[2] Forks only became generally used at table in England during the reign of James I.

Knives are probably the oldest implement of them all. Once crudely fashioned from flint, replaced by iron blades and then crafted in numerous shapes and sizes in bronze, with handles of bone or wood by the Romans.

Keeping Food Warm

One of the earliest known devices for keeping food hot was a crude seventeenth century wrought-iron device shaped like a horseshoe, with upright bars where plates could be stacked, kept warm by being set close to the fireplace. The plates at this time would have been pewter, making them hardier and better able to retain the heat.

By the 1800s, plate warmers had become more sophisticated, as Mrs Beeton explains below:

> In cold weather such joints as venison a haunch saddle or leg of mutton should always be served on a hot water dish as they are so liable to chill This dish is arranged with a double bottom which is filled with very hot water just before the joint is sent to table so keeping that and the gravy deliciously hot Although an article of this description can scarcely be ranked as a kitchen utensil still the utility of it is so obvious that we have thought it would not be out of place to insert an illustration of a dish which it is desirable to possess and which no properly furnished house should be without Price for a dish measuring 16 inches Britannia metal l 18s[3].

As the recruitment of domestic staff began to significantly decline by the beginning of the twentieth century and the female head of middle-class households began to take control of the cooking, it wasn't anticipated how she would also be able to manage the hosting of dinner parties, in addition to the preparation and cooking of the food itself. This problem was rectified during the 1960s, with the invention of that most celebrated of kitsch items, the Hostess Trolley, described here in a 1966 edition of *The Ideal Home Householders' Guide:*

> Most people entertain these days with little or no help in the home and it is most important that the hostess should organise things well beforehand. If not, the guests will only see hasty glimpses of her red face as she trots between them and the kitchen at high speed! It is a good plan to have a dessert that is all ready beforehand and to choose a main dish that can be left to finish itself while the hostess is having a pre-dinner drink with her guests. A trolley is a great help. If one is ready in the kitchen with everything needed for coffee and cheese and biscuits to wind up the meal, it will only take a minute to wheel it into the dining-room.[4]

These heated food cabinets on castors are still manufactured and sold today, although now often as luxury items, in solid wood and brushed steel rather than as every day dinner-party ware. The current John Lewis model retails at a little over £200.

There was an earlier alternative version of the heated hostess trolley. As kitchens were typically situated some distance away from dining rooms, during the nineteenth century warming rooms began to be built adjacent to the dining room. These were small spaces with nothing more than a fire and a steam-heated cabinet, heated by hot water pipes.

Smaller dishes like crumpets and muffins would often be prepared on the fire a little in advance, then kept in special muffin plates that would often be placed over a basin of boiling water.

Preparing the Table

During the Georgian period table displays were often extremely ornamental, always with a centre piece, called a plateau, often of mirrored glass, adorned with sweet meats, fancies, candied and floral flourishes. There would have been a first and then second course, followed by palette cleansers such as confections and cheeses. Within these courses there would be numerous dishes, all laid out on the table.

The great Louis Eustache Ude's early nineteenth century book *The French Cook* offers delightful examples of various Bills of Fare (the one-time name for a Menu). He stipulated that for the first course there must always be a soup, a fish dish, two 'removes' and four entrées. The second course must consist of two roasts, four entremets (small dishes served between courses) and two removes of the roast. 'Removes' refer to the dishes that were prepared and waiting to go out to the table on the sideboard. Two large tureens of soup would usually adorn each end of the dining table, to be replaced by game or meat dishes during the second course. The other dishes would be aligned around the rest of the table on large platters.

It was common practice in Victorian society to display place cards in special holders, handwritten in ink, showing either first names or the full name and title. Fresh flowers were frequently present on the table, with fresh fruits in summer, right up until the end of the Edwardian period. It was also quite typical to provide a menu detailing the courses ahead, to provide some conversation if discussions became dry. At the turn of the twentieth century, small lamps with shades would also be placed on the table to add ambience to the meal.

Plates, Cups and Glasses

Early plates, called trenchers, were used right up until around the eighteenth century and later in some households. These replaced the carved-out slabs of stale bread, originally used to hold food and typically hollowed out by whoever ate from them – guest, or not. There is a trend in some smarter restaurants and gastro pubs today to serve soup and other dishes in this novel way. The wealthier sectors of society would have eaten off pewter.

It was the great potteries of the eighteenth century that would change the fabric of the plate and humble cup forever. 'China' masters like Josiah Wedgwood, Josiah Spode and Thomas Minton capitalised on the fruits of Stoke, creating beautiful coloured, patterned and glazed home wares, classic and stylish, a collector's dream today. The phrase 'china' was adopted after the fashion for imported pottery and ceramics from China that preceded Britain's own mighty production line.

From top to bottom:
Georgian pewter
plate warmer, 1930s;
Burleigh ware and
Victorian Keeling &
Co. lidded tureens;
1940s 'Beryl' ware
sugar bowl and
1930s teapot.
(Emma Kay)

Although plates are integral to our society, cups are even older and more symbolic. Whilst you can always eat off a giant leaf or hunk of wood, a sculptured receptacle for liquid has always been essential – the horn, the shell, and the religious chalice evolved into a variety of drinking vessels for every type of liquid and every occasion. Now there are glasses for red wine, others for white wine, for champagne, for liqueurs, for water, and for juice; cocktail glasses, whiskey tumblers; often within these categories are other categories, like different shaped glasses for different cocktails and specialist sweet desert wine glasses. The list is endless and is worthy of a separate book.

The American fashion for cocktails boomed in Britain during the 1920s and with the cocktail, came the cocktail glass, which quickly became just known as the Martini glass. The first reference I can find to the cocktail glass in Britain was astonishingly as early as 1873 when an article on the popularity of American drinks appeared in the *Edinburgh Evening News*, heralding the new cocktail as 'the American drink par excellence ... made of every imaginable liquor, from gin to champagne...' The article goes on to list some the ingredients and methods involved in mixing cocktails including a whisky sour:

> First squirt some bitters into the tumbler, to which add a little gum for sweetening, and the broken ice; you now put in the whisky, stir up with a spoon to cool it, strain the liquid into a cocktail glass, and drop in a bit of lemon peel. The addition of lime or lemon will make this a 'sour'[5]

By the time enamelling and Bakelite became popular, and cheaper to produce, at the turn of the twentieth century, many specialist glasses became obsolete, except in wealthy society, and the garish plastic cups of the 1960s onwards have morphed into the sort of mass produced, convenient and easy to clean drinking vessels we all use on a daily basis.

Just as I was somewhat shocked to discover that cocktails were being enjoyed in Britain while Queen Victoria was still very much on the throne, I was even more surprised to learn that the first paper cup – largely invented as a consequence of the germ theory and potentially hazardous communal drinking, appeared around the beginning of the 1900s, with experiments to retain boiling water in a paper cups taking place as early as 1901. Whilst the disposable cup was useful, hygienic and cheap, it is clear that it was synonymous with poor quality and shamed a little for its lack of charm, as this 1943 advertisement for *Baker Tailoring* indicates, 'If you wouldn't serve your liquer from a paper cup, you shouldn't trust your clothes to less than the best'.[6]

Condiments

Once again it appears that the Romans, circa 77 CE with their early glass-blowing talents may have invented the first type of cruet with fanciful shaped glass vessels and dishes, filled with culinary liquids carried together in a basket.[7] Novelty cruets were at the height of their popularity between 1890 and 1930, with art deco sets crafted by Clarice Cliff and Susie Cooper being amongst the most valuable to a collector, together with the Carltonware cruet sets of vegetables modelled on a leaf design of the 1950s.

Salt cellars, lidded and unlidded, are perhaps the most curiously fashioned of any item of tableware. From large to small, made from glass, silver, ivory, pewter, wood, ceramic and plastic, they have all been sculptured over the years to suit the period and are often visually reflective of class and personality. Salt cellar is an odd name for a condiment

From top to bottom:
Georgian glass salt
and Edwardian pewter
salt dishes; a pair of
Georgian sauce boats
and vintage cutlery;
Victorian cruet set and
pickle jar. (Emma Kay)

vessel, essentially translating as 'salt-salt', due to the fact that cellar is a corruption of the French word saliere, a salt holder. Ultimately replaced by the mass-produced shakers and grinders of the twentieth century, there is something far more elegant about a small unassuming dish of salt on the table, to be pinched and sprinkled. In 1945 there was a record price obtained for a valuable salt cellar auctioned at Christies; a silver 1549 rarity, it fetched £5,700, a 'pretty penny' for 1945.[8]

Just like the salt cellar, there have been so very many interesting varieties of sugar bowls over time, but perhaps none quite so reassuringly simple in design to me as the ones fashioned from the 'Beryl Ware' range produced by Wood & Sons. Established in the mid-1800s, but unlike so many of their forgotten competitors, they became iconic by the 1940s. The sturdy pale green earthenware range, now so synonymous with wartime collectible kitchenalia boasts cups, saucers, plates, bowls, egg cups, jugs, tea and coffee pots and more besides, including the sugar bowl. Created at a time when Britain's economy was locked down and functionality was far more important than form, Beryl Ware offered pragmatism, yet also a unique sense of understated style and, above all, quality that was absolutely suited to the period.

Sauce boats were highly fashionable in the French court. And as the overwhelming popularity for all things French dominated and influenced British culture during the eighteenth century, French silver sauce boats were copied for the English market then fired into porcelain receptacles by the mid-1700s as the large potteries evolved.[9]

Tureens were also a French influence and during the eighteenth century, these items would become representations of wealth – the more impressive and elaborate the serving dish, the more affluence was credited to its owners.

There are other interesting smaller objects attached to the category of serving, too many to write about here individually, other than to mention corn cob holders, fruit knives, grape scissors, nutcrackers, to name a few. All have their historical place at the table.

Glossary

The following pages provide basic definitions for kitchenalia and kitchen-related items, many of which can be found in this book.

Bath brick   An early scouring/polishing pad for knives, originating from Bridgwater in the South West of England.

'Bully beef'   Term for an early tinned beef used by the British Army. There was a can opener of the same name manufactured by both the English and Americans, in the shape of a bull, complete with horns, eyes and so on.

Biddenden cake mould   Extremely rare moulds of the legendary Chulkhurst twins of Biddenden in Kent, said to have been joined at the hip and shoulder. Cakes or bread were made in the shape of the twins and then doled out to pensioners and the poor every Easter.

Boilers   For boiling large joints of meat. Made of wrought or cast iron

Bottle Jack   For roasting joints on the fire. Wound up, the mechanism turns the meat on a hook below

Chafing dish   From the French to 'make warm'. A portable raised dish heated with charcoal below, to both retain heat and cook food slowly and gently at the table.

Cheese toaster   Mentioned in Mrs Beeton's *Book of Household Management*:

A cheese-toaster with hot-water reservoir: the cheese is melted in the upper tin, which is placed in another vessel of boiling water, so keeping the preparation beautifully hot. A small quantity of porter, or port wine, is sometimes mixed with the cheese; and, if it be not very rich, a few pieces of butter may be mixed with it to great advantage. Sometimes the melted cheese is spread on the toasts, and then laid in the cheese-dish at the top of the hot water. Whichever way it is served, it is highly necessary that the mixture be very hot, and very quickly sent to table, or it will be worthless.

Cook-hold   A two-pronged weapon for fixing meat onto a spit

Dariole/Dariel   A small flowerpot-shaped mould

Digester   Like an early form of pressure cooker, where the steam can only escape through a valve.

Georgian pestle and mortar. (Emma Kay)

Victorian French copper skillet. (Emma Kay)

Docker   A round piece of wood or metal armed with lots of little metal spikes to prick biscuits with and prevent air in the biscuit making it rise when baking.

Dredger   A sift for flour and sugar.

Dutch crowns   Iron hoops fitted with hooks from which to hang meat from the ceiling.

Dutch oven   The original cooking pot, a bit like a witch's cauldron.

Egg slice   A kitchen utensil for removing an omelette or fried egg from the pan.

Firkin   A unit of liquid or a small barrel that fish and butter were stored in and measured by, e.g. a firkin of butter.

Fish kettle and slice   A large pan with a drainer to cook fish, a metal spatula to lift the fish from the kettle.

Gauffre Irons   Tongs to bake small round cakes over the fire.

Gridiron   A cross between a frying-pan and a griddle, square or round with bars or ridges within.

Gum paste board   A board engraved with motifs and patterns to stamp or emboss confectionery, pie or cake decorations.

Hastener   See Meat screen.

Ice-safe   A refrigerator.

Jagger/Jigger   A small wooden tool with a bone, plastic or metal cutting wheel for cutting pastry.

Jelly bag   Felt or flannel bag to strain jellies, purees etc.

Kitchen grease   This was the waste fat from the kitchen. It was an important perk for the cook, since it could be sold for processing into tallow for candles.

Larding needle   To 'sew' fat into the surface of meat.

Lucifer   An early match for lighting fires etc.

Meat safe   Stored in the larder to preserve meats and pastries from flies and dust.

Meat screen   Also known as a Hastener. A contraption in which the joint is hung attached to a jack inside a screen of metal placed in front of the fire. Often fitted with shelves to also warm plates.

Molinillo/Muddler   A turned wooden whisk to stir chocolate.

Nippers   For breaking down lump sugar into smaller pieces

Pantry   A ventilated room, as cold as possible, to store food. Often directly connected to the kitchen.

Parsmint   A French herb mill.

Patty pans   Small tins for baking tarts and cheesecakes.

Peel   A wooden paddle, with a long handle to insert/remove bread from the oven.

Peg and worm   Name given to a travelling or pocket corkscrew. The peg is the handle which fitted into the twist at the end of the screw and was neatly concealed in a little sheath.

Pestle and Mortar   Often in brass, iron, or granite stoneware to pound ingredients such as herbs, spices and meat bones.

Preserving or jam pan   Usually of copper, to make jams, jellies and marmalade by boiling up the fruit.

Pudding cloths   For boiling puddings in.

Salad basket   A wire basket to spin salad in after washing.

Salamander   Essentially a metal plate with a handle designed to be heated and for browning food. When it's hot enough it's held over the food to brown or caramelise it. Sometimes referred to as a grill.

Skillet   Flat-bottom pan for frying.

Skimmer   Large metal spoon with drainage holes, often with a long handle to skim the scum off the surface of milk or cream.

Spice box   A container to hold spices, often with a nutmeg grater at the centre.

Spit   The bar from which a joint of meat is suspended and then turned by hand. A cradle spit is a sort of metal basket that contains the meat while it is being roasted.

Springerle   German biscuit mould.

Spurtle   Scottish stirring spoon.

Steelyard balance or steelyard   A method for weighing. Consists of a straight beam balance and a counterweight that slides along a longer arm to counterbalance the load and gauge the weight.

Tamis or Tammy cloth   A piece of very fine woollen canvas used to strain soups and gravies etc.

Terrine   An earthenware mould, often round, oval or oblong, with a fitted lid to mould coarse pâtés.

Turk's head   A whorled mould resembling a Turkish turban.

Vegetable cutters   Used to stamp vegetables into nice shapes for garnishing purposes.

Notes

Introduction

1. Olsen, K., *Daily Life in 18th Century England*, (Greenwood Publishing, Connecticut and London, 1999)
2. Soyer, A., *The Modern Housewife*, (Simpkin, Marshall & Company, London, 1849)
3. Peel, C.S., *1919 Daily Mail Cookery Book*, (London Associated Newspapers, 1919)
4. Anon *Inquire within for anything you want to know*, (Dick and Fitzgerald, New York, 1858) p.230–232

Storage

1. *The Housekeeping Book of Susanna Whatman*, (Century Hutchinson Ltd, London, 1987), p.53.
2. The British Newspaper Archive, *Caledonian Mercury* (Monday 15 October 1787).
3. The British Newspaper Archive, *Burnley News* (Saturday 09 June 1928).
4. Robertson, J. C., (ed.) *The Mechanics' Magazine, Museum, Register, Journal, and Gazette, Volume 50*, (Robertson and Co, 1849, London).
5. *The Housekeeping Book of Susanna Whatman*, (Century Hutchinson Ltd, London, 1987), p.46.
6. Krutsky, A., 'Spice Boxes', in Fine Woodworking, *Traditional Furniture Projects*, 1991, (Taunton Press, 1991, USA), p.44–45.
7. Davies, J., *The Victorian Kitchen* (BBC Books, 1989, London), p.64.
8. The British Newspaper Archive, *Sunday Post* (22 December, 1946), p.3.
9. Forster, M., *Rich Desserts and Captains Thin* (Vintage Books, London, 2013).
10. Vince, J, *The Country House* (John Murray Ltd, London, 1991), p. 36.
11. Jones, R, *What's Who? A Dictionary of Things Named After People and The People They are Named After*, (Matador Publishing, Leicester, 2009), p.130.
12. I.E.B.C (ed.), *The Country House. A Collection of Useful Information & Recipes* (Horace Cox, London, 1866).

Preparation

1. The British Newspaper Archive, *Dublin Evening Mail*, (Thursday, 13 Feb, 1868), p.1.
2. The British Newspaper Archive, *Aberdeen Journal*, (06 January, 1905), p.3.

3. Kindstedt, P., *Cheese and Culture: A History of Cheese and its Place in Western Civilization,* (Chelsea Green Publishing, 2012), p.88.

4. Bishop, C., *Collecting Kitchenware,* (Millers, London, 1994), p.109.

5. Bishop, C., *Collecting Kitchenware,* (Millers, London, 1994), p.52–53.

6. Bareham, L., *The Trifle Bowl and Other Tales,* (Bantham Press, London, 2013), p.180.

7. Patten, M., *Post-War Kitchen,* (Hamlyn, London, 1998), p.64.

8. University of Nottingham, Dept. of Manuscripts and Special Collections, 'Weights and Measures'[online] (cited 23 May, 2016) Available from https://www.nottingham.ac.uk/manuscriptsandspecialcollections/researchguidance/weightsandmeasures/volumes.aspx,

9. Acton, E., *Modern Cookery for Private Families,* (Longman, Green, Longman, and Roberts, London, 1860), p.260.

10. Webster, T, Parkes, W., *Encyclopaedia of Domestic Economy,* (Harper Brothers, New York, 1855).

11. Nicholl, Fowler., *A Handy Book of Weights and Measures,* (Shaw and Sons, London, 1860), p.97.

12. Bishop, C., *Collecting Kitchenware,* (Millers, London, 1994), p.65.

Dairy

1. *The Farmer's Register,* Volume 2, (1835), p.717.

2. Johnson, C, W., *The Modern Dairy and Cowkeeper,* (J. Ridgway, 1850), p. 97–106.

3. British Newspaper Archive, *The Scotsman,* (24 December, 1917), p.1

4. British Newspaper Archive, *Western Morning News,* (27 September, 1922), p.3.

5. British Newspaper Archive, *Lancashire Evening Post,* (30 December, 1921).

6. British Newspaper Archive, *Dundee Evening Telegraph,* (16 October, 1893).

7. British Newspaper Archive, *Nottingham Evening Post,* (09 December, 1939).

8. British Newspaper Archive, *Daily Gazette for Middlesbrough,* (26 July 1889), p.2.

9. Patten, M., *Post-War Kitchen,* (Hamlyn, London, 1998), p.71

10. British Newspaper Archive, *Evening Despatch* (26 June 1940).

11. Kay, E., *Dining with the Victorians,* (Amberley Publishing, Stroud, 2015), p.41.

12. Bishop, C., *Collecting Kitchenware,* Miller's, London, 1995), p.40–41.

13. British Newspaper Archive, *Western Daily Press,* (10 June, 1924).

14. British Newspaper Archive, *Worcestershire Chronicle,* (10 December, 1881), p.2.

15. Weir, R., 'Mrs. A.B. Marshall, Ice-cream Monger Extraordinary' in H. Walker (ed.) *Cooks and Other People* (Prospect Books, Devon, 1996), p.283.

16. Marshall, A, B., *The Book of Ices,* (Marshall's School of Cookery, London, 1857), p.35.

Drinks

1. 'The Tea Caddy', David McKinley, 2010 [online] (cited 23 May, 2016) Available from http://www.ascasonline.org/articoloMAGGI128.html

2. Dubrin, B., *Tea Culture: History, Traditions, Celebrations, Recipes and More* (Charlesbridge Publishing, USA, 2012), p.35.

3. *Ballou's Dollar Monthly Magazine,* (Boston, 1861), p.187.

4. Hewitt, R., *Coffee Its History, Cultivation, and Uses* (D. Appleton and Company, New York, 1872), p.96–97.

5. Warren, G., *Kitchen Bygones,* (Souvenir Press Ltd, London, 1984), p.42.

6. The British Newspaper Archive, *The Preston Chronicle*, (11 February, 1832) p.2.

7. British Newspaper Archive, *Birmingham Daily Post*, (05 July, 1878), p.6.

8. Kay, E., *Dining with the Georgians*, (Amberley Publishing, Stroud, 2014), p.41–42.

9. Kay, E., *Dining with the Georgians*, (Amberley Publishing, Stroud, 2014), p.51.

10. Kay, E., *Dining with the Georgians*, (Amberley Publishing, Stroud, 2014), p.91.

11. Dickens, C., *A Christmas Carol*, (Ist World Publishing, Fairfield, 2004), p.117.

12. Roberts, G.E., *Cups and Their Customs*, (John Van Voorst, London, 1869), p.41.

13. Roberts, G.E., *Cups and Their Customs*, (John Van Voorst, London, 1869), p,37–38.

Cookware

1. British Newspaper Archive, *Leicester Journal* (21 Feb, 1840), p.3.

2. Jaine, T(ed.)., *Oxford Symposium of Food and Cookery*, The Cooking Medium: Proceedings (Prospect books Ltd, London, 1987), p.111.

3. Beeton, I.M., *The Book of Household Management* (Farrar, Straus, and Giroux, 1861), p.267.

4. *Lloyd's Encyclopædic Dictionary* (1895).

5. Bishop, F., *The illustrated London Cookery Book* (London, 1852) p.298.

6. McWhirther, N., *Norris McWhirter's Book of Millennium Records*, (The Book People, London, 1999).

7. British Newspaper Archive, *Ballymena Observer*, (04 May, 1923), p.8.

8. Rochford, C., *Great Victorian Inventions*, (Amberley Publishing Ltd, Stroud, 2014).

9. Lovelock, J., *Homage to Gaia: The Life of an Independent Scientist*, James Lovelock, Oxford University Press, Oxford, 2001), p.188.

Baking

1. British Newspaper Archive, *Chelmsford Chronicle*, (21 June, 1839).

2. British Newspaper Archive, *Northampton Mercury* (02 April, 1915).

3. Graham, S., *A Treatise on Bread, and Bread Making*, (Light & Stearns, Boston, 1837), p.65.

4. Kay, E., *Dining with the Georgians* (Amberley Publishing Ltd, Stroud, 2014), p.94.

5. David, E *English Bread and Yeast Cookery*, (Penguin, Middlesex, 1979), p. 206–9.

6. British Newspaper Archive, *Portsmouth Evening News*, (09 February, 1923).

7. Foley., *Toys Through the Ages*, (Chilton Books, Philidelphia, 1962).

8. *Simpson's Cookery, Improved and Modernised: The Complete Modern Cook*, (Baldwin and Cradock, London, 1834), p.291.

9. Raffald, E, *Experienced English Housekeeper*, (T. Wilson and. Spence, York, 1806), p.143.

10. Kay, E., *Dining with the Georgians* (Amberley Publishing Ltd, Stroud, 2014), p.74.

11. *Commissioner of Patents Annual Report, 1867*, (Government printing Office, Washington, 1868), p.1434.

12. British Newspaper Archive, *The Evening Chronicle*, (16 May, 1840), p.3.

13. Dickens, C., *Letters on Social Questions. Capital Punishments*, (Daily News, 1846).

Moulds

1. Foley, D., *Toys Through the Ages*, (Chilton Books, Philidelphia, 1962), p.68

2. *German National Cookery for English Kitchens*, 1873 pub Chapman and Hill, London, 1873), p.265.

3. Nicholson, C., *History of Adhesives, Volume 1*, (Bearing Specialists Association, 1991), p.2.
4. Nunn, I., *My Family's Other Recipes: I Didn't Wanna Do It*, (Author House, USA, 2011).
5. Staib, W., *Sweet Taste of History*, (Rowman and Littlefield, USA, 2013), p.88.
6. Massey, J., (1866) *Massey and Son's Biscuit, Ice, & Compote Book* (Simpkin, Marshall, & Co. London, 1866).
7. Francatelli, C.E., *The Modern Cook*, (Richard Bentley, London, 1858).

Utensils
1. Glasse, H., *The Art of Cookery, Made Plain and Easy*, (London, 1774), p.262.
2. Powell, M., *Below Stairs*, (Pan Books, London, 1970), p.51.
3. Beeton, I., *Mrs Beeton's Household Management*, (Wordsworth Editions, Hertfordshire, 2006), p.28.
4. Bouge, D., *French Domestic Cookery*, (London, 1846), p.19–20.
5. Rogers, D., *Inventions and Their Inventors, Volume 1*, (M-Y Books Distribution, 2010).
6. Snodgrass, M.E., *Encyclopaedia of Kitchen History*, (Routledge, London and New York, 2004), p.684.
7. Acton, E., *Modern Cookery for Private Families*, (Longman, Green, Longman, and Roberts, London, 1860), p.182.
8. Dirck, B., *Lincoln the Lawyer* (University of Illinois, Chicago, 2008), p.89.
9. *The Farmer's Magazine*, (Rogerson and Tuxford, London, 1861), p.348.
10. Snodgrass, M.E., *Encyclopaedia of Kitchen History*, (Routledge, London and New York, 2004), p.658.
11. British Newspaper Archive, *Nottingham Evening Post*, (11 July, 1950), p.3.
12. Soyer, A., *Gastronomic Regenerator*, (Simpkin, Marshall & Company, London, 1847).
13. Stefferud, A., *Yearbook of Agriculture*, (US Government Printing Office, USA, 1894), p.130.
14. British Newspaper Archive *Birmingham Daily Post* (29 March, 1890), p.1.
15. May, R., *The Accomplished Cook* (N. Brooke, London, 1671), p.235.

Serving
1. Drachenfels, S.V., *The Art of the Table: A Complete Guide to Table Setting*, (Simon and Schuster, New York, 2000).
2. *House & Garden, Volume 10* (1906), p.177.
3. Beeton, I.M., *The Englishwoman's Cookery Book*, (Ward, Lock and Tyler, London, 1872).
4. *Ideal Home Householders Guide, Volume 3*, (1966), p.194.
5. British Newspaper Archive, *Edinburgh Evening News*, (24 September, 1873), p.4.
6. British Newspaper Archive, *Hartlepool Northern Daily Mail*, (06 April, 1943).
7. Snodgrass, M.E., *Encyclopaedia of Kitchen History*, (Routledge, Oxford, 2004).
8. British Newspaper Archive, *Western Daily Press*, (16 July, 1945), p.
9. Steen, J., *The Kitchen Magpie: A delicious melange of culinary curiosities, fascinating facts, amazing anecdotes and expert tips for the food-lover*, (Icon Books Ltd, 2014).

Bibliography

Acton, E., *Modern Cookery for Private Families*, (Longman, Green, Longman, and Roberts, London, 1860).

Anon Inquire within for anything you want to know, (Dick and Fitzgerald, New York, 1858)

Ballou's Dollar Monthly Magazine, (Boston, 1861).

Bareham, L., *The Trifle Bowl and Other Tales*, (Bantham Press, London, 2013).

Beeton, I.M., *The Book of Household Management*, (Farrar, Straus, and Giroux, 1861)

Beeton, I.M., *The Englishwoman's Cookery Book*, (Ward, Lock and Tyler, London).

Beeton, I., *Mrs Beeton's Household Management*, (Wordsworth Editions, Hertfordshire).

Bishop, C., *Collecting Kitchenware*, (Millers, London, 1994).

Bishop, F., *The illustrated London Cookery Book*, (London, 1852).

Bouge, D., *French Domestic Cookery*, (London, 1846).

British Newspaper Archive, Birmingham Daily Post (29 March, 1890).

British Newspaper Archive, Aberdeen Journal, (06 January, 1905).

British Newspaper Archive, Ballymena Observer, (04 May, 1923).

British Newspaper Archive, Birmingham Daily Post, (05 July, 1878).

British Newspaper Archive, Burnley News (Saturday 09 June, 1928).

British Newspaper Archive, Caledonian Mercury (Monday 15 October, 1787).

British Newspaper Archive, Daily Gazette for Middlesbrough, (26 July, 1889).

British Newspaper Archive, Dublin Evening Mail, (Thursday, 13 Feb, 1868).

British Newspaper Archive, Dundee Evening Telegraph, (16 October, 1893).

British Newspaper Archive, Edinburgh Evening News, (24 September, 1873), p.4

British Newspaper Archive, Evening Despatch (26 June, 1940).

British Newspaper Archive, Hartlepool Northern Daily Mail, (06 April, 1943).

British Newspaper Archive, Lancashire Evening Post, (30 December, 1921).

British Newspaper Archive, Leicester Journal (21 Feb, 1840).

British Newspaper Archive, Nottingham Evening Post, (09 December, 1939).

British Newspaper Archive, Nottingham Evening Post, (11 July, 1950).

British Newspaper Archive, Sunday Post (22 December, 1946).

British Newspaper Archive, The Preston Chronicle, (11 February, 1832).

British Newspaper Archive, The Scotsman, (24 December, 1917).

British Newspaper Archive, Western Daily Press, (10 June, 1924).

British Newspaper Archive, Western Daily Press, (16 July, 1945).

British Newspaper Archive, Western Morning News, (27 September, 1922).

British Newspaper Archive, Worcestershire Chronicle, (10 December, 1881).

Davies, J., *The Victorian Kitchen*, (BBC Books, 1989, London).

Dickens, C., *A Christmas Carol*, (Ist World Publishing, Fairfield, 2004).

Dirck, B., *Lincoln the Lawyer*, (University of Illinois, Chicago, 2008).

Drachenfels, S.V., *The Art of the Table: A Complete Guide to Table Setting*, (Simon and Schuster, New York, 2000).

Dubrin, B., *Tea Culture: History, Traditions, Celebrations, Recipes and More*, (Charles Bridge Publishing, USA, 2012).

Foley, D., *Toys Through the Ages*, (Chilton Books, Philidelphia, 1962).

Forster, M., *Rich Desserts and Captains Thin*, (Vintage Books, London, 2013).

Francatelli, C.E., *The Modern Cook*, (Richard Bentley, London, 1858).

German National Cookery for English Kitchens, (Chapman and Hill, London, 1873).

Glasse, H., T*he Art of Cookery, Made Plain and Easy*, (London, 1774).

Hewitt, R., *Coffee Its History, Cultivation, and Uses*, (D. Appleton and Company, New York, 1872).

House & Garden, Volume 10 (1906).

I.E.B.C (ed.), *The Country House. A Collection of Useful Information & Recipes*, (Horace Cox, London, 1866).

Ideal Home Householders Guide, Volume 3, (1966).

Jaine, T., (ed.), *Oxford Symposium of Food and Cookery, The Cooking Medium: Proceedings*, (Prospect books Ltd, London, 1987).

Johnson, C.W., *The Modern Dairy and Cowkeeper*, (J. Ridgway, 1850

Kay, E., *Dining with the Georgians*, (Amberley, Gloucestershire, 2014).

Kay, E., *Dining with the Victorians*, (Amberley, Gloucestershire, 2015).

Kindstedt, P., *Cheese and Culture: A History of Cheese and its Place in Western Civilization*, (Chelsea Green Publishing, 2012).

Krutsky, A., 'Spice Boxes', in *Fine Woodworking, Traditional Furniture Projects*, 1991, (Taunton Press, 1991, USA).

Lloyd's Encyclopædic Dictionary (1895).

Lovelock, J., *Homage to Gaia: The Life of an Independent Scientist, James Lovelock*, (Oxford University Press, Oxford, 2001).

Marshall, A, B., *The Book of Ices*, (Marshall's School of Cookery, London, 1857).

Massey, J., *Massey and Son's Biscuit, Ice, & Compote Book* (Simpkin, Marshall, & Co. London, 1866).

May, R., *The Accomplished Cook* (N. Brooke, London, 1671), p.235.

McWhirther, N., *Norris McWhirter's Book of Millennium Records*, (The Book People, London, 1999).

Nicholl, J., Fowler., *A Handy Book of Weights and Measures*, (Shaw and Sons, London, 1860).

Nicholson, C., *History of Adhesives, Volume 1*, (Bearing Specialists Association, 1991).

Nunn, I., *My Family's Other Recipes: I Didn't Wanna Do It*, (Author House, USA, 2011).

Olsen, K., *Daily Life in 18th Century England*, (Greenwood Publishing, Connecticut and London, 1999).

Patten, M., *Post-War Kitchen*, (Hamlyn, London, 1998).

Peel, C.S., *1919 Daily Mail Cookery Book*, (London Associated Newspapers, 1919).

Powell, M., *Below Stairs*, (Pan Books, London, 1970).

Roberts, G.E., *Cups and Their Customs*, (John Van Voorst, London, 1869).

Robertson. J.C., (ed.), *The Mechanics' Magazine, Museum, Register, Journal, and Gazette, Volume 50*, (Robertson and Co, 1849, London).

Rochford, C., *Great Victorian Inventions*, (Amberley Publishing Ltd, Stroud, 2014).

Rogers, D., *Inventions and Their Inventors, Volume 1*, (M-Y Books Distribution, 2010).

Snodgrass, M.E., *Encyclopaedia of Kitchen History*, (Routledge, London and New York, 2004).

Soyer, A., *Gastronomic Regenerator*, (Simpkin, Marshall & Company, London, 1847).

Soyer, A., *The Modern Housewife*, (Simpkin, Marshall & Company, London, 1849)

Staib, W., *Sweet Taste of History*, (Rowman and Littlefield, USA, 2013)

Steen, J., *The Kitchen Magpie: A delicious melange of culinary curiosities, fascinating facts, amazing anecdotes and expert tips for the food-lover*, (Icon Books Ltd, 2014).

Stefferud, A., *Yearbook of Agriculture*, (US Government Printing Office, USA, 1894), p.130.

The Farmer's Magazine, (Rogerson and Tuxford, 1861, London), p.348.

The Farmer's Register, Volume 2, (1835), p.717.

The Housekeeping Book of Susanna Whatman, (Century Hutchinson Ltd, London, 1987).

The Tea Caddy', David McKinley, 2010 [online] (cited 23 May, 2016) Available from http://www.ascasonline.org/articoloMAGGI128.html

University of Nottingham, Dept. of Manuscripts and Special Collections, 'Weights and Measures' [online] (cited 23 May, 2016) Available from https://www.nottingham.ac.uk/manuscriptsandspecialcollections/researchguidance/weightsandmeasures/volumes.aspx,

Vince, J, *The Country House* (John Murray Ltd, London, 1991).

Warren, G., *Kitchen Bygones*, (Souvenir Press Ltd, London, 1984).

Webster, T., Parkes, W., *Encyclopaedia of Domestic Economy*, (Harper Brothers, New York, 1855).

Weir, R., 'Mrs. A.B. Marshall, Ice-cream monger Extraordinary' in H. Walker (ed.) *Cooks and Other People*, (Prospect Books, Devon, 1996).